LET'S CELEBRATE

LET'S CELEBRATE

Through the Church's Year in the family

Tony Castle

HODDER AND STOUGHTON
LONDON   SYDNEY   AUCKLAND   TORONTO

The author and publishers would like to thank the *Catholic Gazette* for permission to reproduce 'A Missionary I know'. Scripture quotations are from the *Jerusalem Bible*, published and copyright © 1966, 1967 and 1968 by Darton, Longman and Todd Ltd., and Doubleday & Co., Inc., used by permission of the publishers.

British Library Cataloguing in Publication Data

Castle, Tony
   Let's celebrate.
   1. Family—Religious life
   I. Title
   249   BV4526.2

ISBN 0 340 34245 5

*To Peter and Christine,
my brother and sister,
and their families*

Contents

Foreword

Tony Castle says that the inspiration for this book came from Pope John Paul's exhortation to the Catholics of Britain that their homes should be 'centres of prayer where families are at ease in the presence of God'. This may sound like a high ideal, but this book provides the means for any family to make this a reality.

What particularly appeals to me is that this is not just another family prayer book, but a book that brings the prayer at the heart of the church and its liturgy right into the home, giving even the youngest members of a family access to its teaching and truth.

This is an important book because we live in an age when children are exposed more than ever to the world of unbelief and its values. So many children suffer from over-stimulation and have never learned the value of just a few moments pause for reflection.

This book will help parents remedy that, and create an atmosphere where children are encouraged to learn about the deeper meaning of life, and – together with their parents – to seek, to know and to respond to God. If you are a parent who needs help with this, that help is now at hand.

Delia Smith

Introduction

Modern trends in kitchen design seem to be against kitchen tables but I find them a great institution. Where they exist they become one of the principal focal points of the home: Mums prepare meals on them; grandmothers sit at them to give advice; children draw and paint on them; familiar visitors share them as they share a mug of coffee and the local news. And, perhaps most important of all, lots of families have their meals round them.

This book is the product of our kitchen table! I have a study – no more immune from the noise of the children than the kitchen – but it felt right and natural to put this book together at the site of much family sharing, prayer and celebration. Of course that had to happen before the children got up in the morning or after they had reluctantly retired!

While the meal table is the gathering point for the family, the altar in our parish church is the focal point for the family of God each Sunday. That weekly gathering, to share the word of God and the sacrificial meal, is to recall and celebrate the first Easter. Although the purpose of this book is to help families understand and celebrate all the seasons and festivals of the Church's year, the reader will find that one event is constantly being referred to, directly and indirectly, an event which overshadows every other day in the year: the resurrection of the Lord. No other event demonstrates so vividly or dramatically the immeasurable love of Jesus; no other event shows more clearly the re-creation work of the Father and Holy Spirit. It is THE event upon which the whole of our Faith is founded: 'And if Christ has not been raised then our preaching is useless and your believing it is useless' (1 Cor. 15:14).

The idea for this book came from Pope John Paul's words about the family, on his historic visit to Britain:

'May your homes become schools of prayer for both parents and children'. (At Wembley Stadium.)

'I urge that your homes be centres of prayer; homes where families are at ease in the presence of God'. (At York.)

He voiced a beautiful ideal that needs interpreting and translating into practical everyday action. Following the Church's year, which, with its colour and variety covers all the key truths of our Faith, is the most effective way for the family to do this. If at times this book seems to present high ideals it is quite intentional because unless we reach up from our daily mundane lives the Pope's exhortation will remain an empty dream.

I would like at this point to draw attention to what this book is not. It is not intended to be read from cover to cover, but rather to be dipped into. For example, at the beginning of Advent or Lent parents might like to read the appropriate chapter, looking for ways to enliven the season in the home. Some of what they read might be put into action at once, other ideas the family might have to 'grow' towards, little by little, as time passes.

It is important to stress that this book does not spring from the ideal family that already puts all these suggestions and plans into practice. Our children are still very young, which means they are more amenable to the projects and little services that we have tried than older children might be. Some ideas have been gleaned from our friends who have used them for some time, others we hope one day to use as we annually live out the Church's year in the home.

I would like to thank Delia Smith for so kindly writing the foreword, Arthur Baker for the drawings with the professional touch, my seven-year-old daughter Helena for the homely amateur drawings, Father Harry Stratton for his words of advice and Sheila Taylor for her hard work at the typewriter.

THE COMING OF LOVE

'Hurry up, we'll be late.'

'I'll have to run if I'm going to catch the 8.05!'

'Peter's got to be at five-a-side at six o'clock; Chris has got ballet at six-thirty.'

We are creatures ruled by time. We 'take' it, 'save' it, 'spend' it, 'waste' it. Time moves relentlessly on with measured pace; yet when we are happy it seems to fly and when we are miserable it appears to drag.

This ancient little verse can be seen in Chester cathedral:

When as a child I laughed and wept – time crept.
When as a youth I dreamed and talked – time
    walked.
When I became a full-grown man – time ran.
And later as I older grew – time flew.
Soon I shall find while travelling on – time gone.
Will Christ have saved my soul by then? Amen.

TIME LIMITS US

It is often said that 'time is money'. Much more serious than that, time is life. For as the minutes tick by we become progressively older; our lives tick by. To use time well is to live our lives well, to waste time is to waste that which is most precious of all to us, our lives.

Occasionally we stop and look at our children, or find an old photo of them, and then we realise how they've grown. With that realisation comes the thought that we too are getting older. When we in turn take a look at our parents (if they are still with us) we see what time is doing to them. We are sadly reminded of the shortness of life and how limiting it is.

God has no limits. He's very lucky, He doesn't grow old. Minutes, hours, days, weeks, months, even hundreds of passing years have no effect upon Him, He is outside of time. We start a new calendar year on 1st January. It has meaning for us, but not for God. Every day is NOW for Him. We start a new Church year with the first Sunday of Advent, but still it has no effect upon God. It is still NOW for Him. Even the Church's holy seasons do not do anything to or for God. The Church's year is for our benefit, to help us draw closer in love and service to the Father, through the Son by the power of the Holy Spirit.

Gloucester cathedral has a sundial with these words on it:

Give God thy heart, thy service and thy gold;
The day wears on and time is waxing old.

Time started when God decided to create; before that there was no time. The motion of God's creation, the sun, planets and the earth with its moon, makes time. So creation and time are interwoven. The moment God said, 'Let there be light,' time began and has flowed on ever since. The twelve months of our calendar, from January to December, measure that time.

The Church's year begins with 'the coming' or 'Advent' as it is called. It is a title that implies a passing of time, a period of expectation and hope. It is the season of the Church's year which is most concerned with 'time'.

LOVE IS GOD

Just as we can't talk about 'the year' without speaking about 'time', so we can't think about 'the family' and family life without considering 'love'. And that word is probably the most used and abused in the English language:

- the child says, 'I love bananas.'
- the romantic novel tells of 'the love in her eyes'.
- the Jewish proverb says, 'Love your neighbour even when he plays the trombone.'
- the husband says to his wife, 'I love you.'
- the Apostle John tells us that 'God is love'.

Surely the greatest revelation of the Good News from Jesus was this, that 'God is love' (1 John 4:16). We may *have* a preference for bananas, or *have* an emotional affection for a friend, or a desire to respect our neighbour. But while we *have* such a love, God *is* love.

Genuine human love is a share, in some mysterious and wonderful way, in that love which *is* God. For example, when a couple fall in love and have that 'swept-off-your-feet' experience, they are immersed in a love which is a share in God's love. Assuming a couple want to express this love in the gift of themselves to one another in marriage, they move even closer to God when they make that commitment. It is the beginning of a life of commitments in and through the family. And God is continually looking for such expressions of love from us: 'if you love me,' Jesus said, in John's gospel 'you will do what I ask (John 15:10). Marriage is a total commitment in love.

LOVE MADE VISIBLE

The loving gift of one person to another, helping the marriage to grow in maturity, can produce the visible sign and expression of their love – the new baby. Pope John Paul II has called the family 'a community of love'. It is a community that starts with a 'falling in love' and grows to maturity through the physical sexual expression of that love.

There's a saying that goes, 'A new baby is God's sign that He wants His world to continue.' God did not stop creating at the beginning of the world; He goes on and on, every minute of every day, expressing His love, in time, through the love of parents for one another. Parents work with God in the passing on of life. They are co-creators with God – God needs loving parents. Love is absolutely essential for each of us. Unless there is a loving atmosphere in which the child can learn to receive and give love he will never grow to full and proper maturity.

Some years ago the following story appeared in one of our national papers:

Kevin, a ten-year-old from the country, came to spend the Easter holidays with his aunt who lived in the London suburb of Wimbledon. Curious to explore not only her large garden but also an overgrown path at the back, he heard odd noises coming from a shed in a neighbour's garden. When he asked his aunt about the noise she told him that she thought her unmarried lady neighbour kept chickens. Kevin had been brought up on a chicken farm and knew immediately that what he had heard was not 'chicken-noise'. He went back through a hole in the fence to investigate. The neighbouring garden was very overgrown but with a clear path running from the house to the old shed. The shed door was padlocked and the window was blacked out but there was a large sort of letter-box slit in the door.

First checking that no one was watching, Kevin peeped through the 'letter-box'. It was covered on the inside by a piece of hanging material but a powerful stench caught Kevin's nose. Just as he was about to turn away the cover was lifted and a pair of wild staring eyes appeared at the slit. Kevin gave a startled scream and bolted out of the garden back to his aunt's. He ran straight into her. He was so upset that he blurted out just what he had seen. His aunt called the police.

The dignified maiden lady was very indignant at first when the police asked to inspect her garden shed. When they insisted, her resistance collapsed and she gave them a key. On opening the shed door a sight met the eyes of the two constables that they are never likely to forget. Cowering in a darkened corner from the bright light and the strange intruders was the naked figure of what seemed to be a strange animal. It was on all fours and had long black hair. There was fear in the wild eyes and 'it' made strange little noises. The police officers, taken aback by the sight and the stench, closed the door again and radioed for assistance.

The nine-year-old boy was taken into very special care. He had been in the shed for seven years, since the age of two, when the woman, fearing the discovery of her secret illegitimate child, had incarcerated him in the shed. Besides the filth, long hair and nails his back was bent in such a way that he would never be able to learn to walk upright. Terrified at the presence of other people, he could not communicate but merely express emotions by grunts. He had never known any caring love and there was no hope of a return to full human existence.

This extreme case shows most dramatically what happens to a work of God's creation if there is no caring love. And if there are no parents, or parent, to give time to teaching a child how to walk, how to speak and how to learn from play and family example. The less love there is in a human's life the more like an animal that person becomes; the more genuine unselfish love there is, the nearer the person comes to God. Without caring love children cannot grow to full maturity.

GOD STEPS INTO TIME

At a moment in history there was a great meeting between 'Time' and 'Love' and the result was a weak helpless baby. When God came into our world that's how he came. On the first Christmas night the Son of God, 'Love' itself, became one of us.

Our annual celebration of that great event needs to be prepared for.

THE 'COMING' SEASON

In the Church's season of 'the coming', we find not one meeting of 'Love' and 'Time' prepared for and celebrated, but three. The liturgy of Advent speaks of the three 'comings' of Jesus. This can be a little confusing, unless clearly spelt out and thought about:

(1) The coming of 'Love' as a baby – the first coming of Jesus as a member of a family.

(2) The coming of 'Love' as the Word of God – the second coming of Jesus at the age of 30 as a preacher.

(3) The coming of 'Love' as the judge – the final coming of Christ at the end of time as our judge.

In the four weeks of Advent these three 'comings' of Jesus are recalled. It is a time to consider their importance for us.

In family life so much is learnt in an accumulative way, by the constant repeating of advice or a good habit. That's the way children learn how to behave. It's the same in the family of the Church. The Church's year, like Nature's seasons, comes round again and again. We do not need to be anxious about doing and learning everything at once. The repetition has an effect and the influence builds up over the years. How then can we best use the time of Advent to grow in knowledge and love of God? Here are a number of practical suggestions.

Advent Resolutions. A new year, a new beginning and an ideal opportunity to make a fresh start or at least a special effort. If giving time to our children is a mark of our love for them, so too giving time to God is an expression of love. For centuries Christians have used Advent and Lent to make a renewed effort at building a closer relationship with Christ. Simple, not-too-difficult-to-fulfil resolutions help to keep the family on course for a more satisfying celebration of Our Lord's birthday and all that it implies for us. If prayer has been neglected in the family, now is the chance to make a new start; if some of the following ideas seem attractive and feasible, now is the opportunity to introduce a few of them (more can be added next time Advent comes round!).
Beware! During our season of Advent the commercial world is trying hard to 'sell' Christmas to the shopper. Their interest in Christmas closes with the shops on Christmas Eve. That's when for us Advent ends and we begin to celebrate Christmas, a celebration that runs on until 6th January and the feast of the Epiphany.

Advent Calendar. Of all the aids to mark the 'coming' feature of this religious season the Advent calendar is the best known and most widely used. While these calendars with their step by step approach to Christmas have become more and more popular, most of those for sale in the shops have lost their original meaning and purpose. To be a proper 'coming' calendar it should count off the days to the Christ child's birth with a growing sense of wonder and excitement. The overall picture, before the little windows are opened, should not be of Father Christmas nor should it be a nativity scene. The first has no immediate connection with Advent and the second totally destroys the sense of 'coming'. The scene should 'unfold' gradually, with only the final picture revealing the true meaning of Christmas.

The primary, overall picture for a proper calendar will have, for example, a village scene – Bethlehem – with people going about their everyday work. (Avoid 'glitter' and 'tinsel' pictures because they give completely the wrong impression. There was no glitter about Christ's birth; he came into a very ordinary village scene.) As the 'windows' are opened more and more of the life of the village is revealed. Until finally on the twenty-fourth the nativity scene is revealed. There's no need to buy a new one every year. Once a really good one has been found it can be used again and again (as long as the windows can be folded back and not torn out!).

The daily 'opening' should be by one of the children, taking it in turns. Breakfast is a good time. It's an ideal opportunity for the supervising adult to say just a word or two about the passing of time, mentioning perhaps the long period of waiting by the Jewish people before the Messiah was born, or how ordinary life was going on in Bethlehem, but there was the Son of God in the midst of it all, and so on. An enterprising family can make their own attractively different calendar.

Beware! For convenience Advent calendars begin on 1st December. In reality Advent begins two or three days before that, so the calendar does *not* begin on the first day of Advent.

Advent Wreath. Wreaths, in Ancient Greece, were hung by young people on their lover's door as a sign of affection. Throughout history they have regularly been used to signify honour and joy. An Advent wreath differs from a decorative wreath of holly leaves, evergreens, berries, etc., by having four candles standing upright and representing the four Sundays of Advent.

The wreath can either be hung by ribbons, for example from a light fixture in the middle of the room, or more safely these days, act as a table decoration. It can reside on a sideboard or dresser during the week and be given the place of honour in the centre of the dining-room table on a Sunday.

There are various ways of making a wreath. Here are a few suggestions that might help.

a)   This is probably the simplest method. Cut out a circle of cardboard about 8 inches in diameter (you can get one out of a large cornflakes packet), make a two-inch hole in the centre and cover it with silver cooking-foil. Give it a thick edge of evergreen, holly, ivy, etc., which can be attached through the cardboard with fuse wire. A few little red bows can be added to give a dash of colour and four large blobs of Blu-Tack or Plasticine placed equal distances apart on the inside edge to push the four red candles into. Symbols (see p 28 on the Jesse Tree and Advent House) can, if desired, be fashioned out of white pipe-cleaners and placed in turn, one each week, flat in the centre.

b)   Two old wire coathangers are very useful for the foundation of a larger, more solid wreath. Pull the bottom straight lengths out until they are bowed, then lap them over one another so that the top of each hook just touches the 'bow' of the other hanger (see picture). Now wire them together with fuse wire.

Cover the frame with a strip of material (a redundant sheet, perhaps), then a circle of evergreen. Fit candle-holders made from screw-on bottle tops into the four angles made by the overlapping hangers. Decorate with little red bows or suitable small artificial flowers.

c)   A more substantial wreath can be constructed from a circle of wire netting (the sort that is used for rabbit hutches). The candle holders can be forced into the already existing holes which of course can also hold the evergreen.

The Advent wreath is rich in symbolism which can be explained step by step to the children as they help make it.

The circle is a symbol of eternity – time without end. As you can go round and round the circle without coming to an end so time with God goes on and on. This is the never-endingness of God.

Evergreens stand for eternal life, life without end. Evergreens don't die in the winter and like them God is always fresh and new – He never withers and dies. We were born to live forever with Him.

Candles remind us of Christ the 'light of the world'. We are also reminded of the big candle at church blessed during the Easter vigil; small ones were given to us at our baptism. A writer of the early years of Christianity, Tertullian, said of Christians, 'you are a light of the world; a tree evergreen.'

Four candles represent the four weeks of Advent. Each
  Sunday we light a new candle as the celebration of
  Christ's coming gets ever nearer.
Beware! With children around lit candles should never
  be left unattended.

Using the Advent wreath as a centre-piece table decoration and lighting a candle before, during or after the grace
before Sunday dinner, when the whole family are present,
would seem to be the best way to use it. (If it is hung up
somewhere in the house it is not so accessible to the
children.) Children love lighting candles and, of course,
need to be supervised with care – they also like blowing
them out! As far as age permits everyone should get a
'turn' in lighting and blowing out. (There are ten 'light-
ings' so there's plenty of opportunity for all.) The grace
before the meal should mention, if possible, the Coming of
Christ, and as that Sunday's candle is lit the person
lighting can say, 'Come, Lord Jesus, light of the world,' or
'The light of Christ.'

Advent Candle. As an alternative to the calendar and the
wreath it is possible to make or buy a large candle with the
numbers 1–24 running down the side of it. This too can
best be used as a table decoration and lit at the principal
meal each day. For its symbolism to have any value the
lighting of the candle each day should be accompanied by
a prayer, perhaps as above.

The 'O' Prayers. In the Church's liturgy, special sung
prayers called antiphons have played a part for many
centuries in the preparation for Christmas. They were
called the great 'O' antiphons because each one began
with an 'O'. Beginning on 17th December the ancient Old
Testament titles of the coming Messiah are used in this
prayer of the Church. The first addresses the Word of God
as, 'O Wisdom' (O Sapientia). The second title links up

with Moses (O Adonai) 'O Lord of Lords'. The third refers to Jesse, who was the father of David, and of course Jesus was of the House of David and born in David's town of Bethlehem: 'O Root of Jesse' (O Radix Jesse). The next antiphon uses the title 'Key of David' (Clavis David) and refers to the kingly authority associated with David. The next one, 'O Rising Dawn' (O Oriens), speaks of the coming Messiah as the light of the world. The antiphon for the 22nd December, 'O Rex Gentium' (King of Nations), stresses that the Messiah is not for the Jews alone, but the whole human race. The final antiphon, 'O Emmanuel', uses the very special title which describes most exactly the role of the expected Messiah, 'God-with-us'.

The 'coming' period comes to a beautiful climax with these prayers rooted in the Scriptures, all of which end with an appeal for the Christ to 'come'. While perhaps not suitable as table prayers (see page 67) with very young children, they could easily and profitably be used where family members are more mature. Naturally they would need some explanation, particularly when first introduced.

December 17th

WISDOM

O Wisdom, you come forth from the mouth of the Most High. You fill the universe and hold all things together in a strong yet gentle manner. O come to teach us the way of truth.

December 18th

LORD OF LORDS

O Lord of lords and leader of Israel, you appeared to Moses in a burning bush and you gave him the Law on Sinai. O come and save us with your mighty power.

December 19th

ROOT OF JESSE

O root of Jesse, you stand as a signal for the nations; kings fall silent before you whom the peoples acclaim. O come to deliver us, and do not delay.

December 20th

KEY OF DAVID

O key of David and sceptre of Israel, what you open no one else can close again; what you close no one can open. O come to lead the captive from prison; free those who sit in darkness and in the shadow of death.

December 21st

RISING SUN

O Rising Sun, you are the splendour of eternal light and the sun of justice. O come and enlighten those who sit in darkness and in the shadow of death.

December 22nd

KING OF NATIONS

O King of the nations, whom all desire, you are the cornerstone which makes all one. O come and save man whom you made from clay.

December 23rd

GOD WITH US

O Emmanuel, you are our king and judge, the one whom the peoples await and their saviour. O come and save us, Lord, our God.

Advent House. This is a similar idea to the calendar and it is made in the same way. However, unlike the calendar it covers only the last seven days of Advent and not the whole period. The children can copy and decorate (to a uniform size) the seven symbols suggested by the anti-phons shown above. These are positioned and glued to a sheet of paper measuring approximately 12 inches by 9 inches. Another sheet, which is to be the top sheet of the two and a little larger than the first one, is drawn and coloured as the front of a house with roof, door, and seven windows. Over the door, with a little decoration, can be written the words 'House of David'. The windows are scored down one side and are cut to hinge open (just like the Advent calendar) but the actual opening is left until the appropriate day.

If you are going to use this idea it is important that the symbols are explained to the children while they are copying and colouring them. There may be an opportunity to give another word of explanation, or encourage an older child to explain, as the windows are bent back and the symbols are revealed. A few words are also necessary about the 'House of David', carefully explaining that a building is not literally meant.

Jesse Tree. The Christmas tree is a well established part of the family Christmas, but it has no religious connection with the festival. It's well known that Queen Victoria's consort, Albert, brought the custom over from Germany. It seems to have become part of Christmas there through a link with the German mystery plays of the Middle Ages. In those plays the evergreen fir tree was used to stand for the tree of good and evil in the garden of paradise.

In other parts of Europe during the Middle Ages another kind of tree was being linked with Christmas, the Jesse tree. Although they were fairly common at that time in the stained glass window designs of many cathedrals and churches, examples can now only be seen in a few places, namely Wells Cathedral, Dorchester Abbey and St George's, Hanover Square, London (see page 116). The stained glass design is based upon the Bible text, 'There shall come forth . . . out of his root'. (This of course links up with the 'O' antiphon we have just talked about.) The windows show a tree, the roots being Jesse, the father of King David, then the people and events between him and Jesus portrayed symbolically as fruit at the top.

The ordinary family Christmas tree can be dressed up as a Jesse tree. The children may copy and then decorate cut-out pictures of symbols representing the people or events that prepared the way, through the Old Testament, for the coming of Jesus. Those who use this method to make their Christmas tree fulfil a religious role in the run-up to Christmas use symbols from throughout the Old Testament and not just from King David's time onwards. For example, creation can be symbolised by a cut-out sun and moon, the fall of Adam and Eve by an apple. A cardboard ark can be used for Noah and family, a bundle of sticks for Isaac, a ladder for Jacob, a harp for King David, and so on. It is certainly an excellent way of helping the children to think about the people of the Old Testament. Bible colouring books, which can be purchased in Christian bookshops around the country, can be invaluable as a basis for the decoration and colouring.

An Advent Blessing. We always think of 'blessings' as part of the work of the priest, but in fact *asking* a blessing – as distinct from *giving* a blessing – is something anyone can do. Grace before meals is precisely that, asking God to bless the food and the meal.

If it can be arranged, a little simple ceremony asking God's blessing on the wreath, calendar, house or tree helps to highlight the purpose of the project and set it aside as something more than a plaything. Nothing elaborate or demanding is required; simplicity is best. It should only take place when the whole family can be present. Then one parent can, after the sign of the cross, say a prayer similar to the following:

> Heavenly Father, we are getting ready now to celebrate the coming of your Son among us. We ask you to bless this wreath (calendar/house) that we have made (decorated) to help us prepare well for Christmas. Bless too our family and all those we love. We ask you this through Jesus your Son.
>
> Amen.

The Lord's prayer said together, and/or the Hail Mary, can fill out and conclude the little ceremony. If the calendar or house is involved then the first window could now be opened.

ST NICHOLAS' DAY, 6TH DECEMBER

Some Christian families have a problem about Santa Claus or Father Christmas. They feel there is a conflict between the real meaning of Christmas and the Father Christmas myth. This shouldn't be a problem for Catholic families with a traditional reverence for the saints of God. 'Santa Claus' is a name which has been broken down through regular use from 'Sinter Claes', which is the Dutch for Saint Nicholas. It has entered into the English language through the Dutch settlers that went and set up home in North America.

Saint Nicholas lived around the fourth century and was probably the Bishop of Myra (a town which would nowadays be in modern Turkey). His existence is only known through traditional stories. It seems that after being born in Turkey he travelled widely and suffered imprisonment for his faith under the Emperor Diocletian. He was famous – so tradition has it – for his loving concern for the needy, and especially children and young people. There are many legends that tell of his generosity, but the best known one is of the three marriageable young girls who could not marry because their parents were too poor to provide them with a dowry. Hearing of their plight Bishop Nicholas secretly, one night, left a bag of gold at their house for the eldest daughter. Not long afterwards she found a husband. Later Nicholas crept by a second time and dropped another bag of gold through their window. The second daughter soon married. As he was about to deliver the third gift, the father caught sight of him. The traditional story closes with the grateful father throwing himself at Saint Nicholas' feet, thanking him for his generosity.

Obviously this story is the basis of the Santa Claus tradition which made its way into the English Christmas from the New Amsterdam (New York) Dutch who developed the traditional story into the form we now have it.

A St Nicholas Service

The parish (and school) and family can come together to celebrate the feast of Saint Nicholas in such a way that the Santa Claus connection with Christmas can be explained. In one parish, for example, each year on 6th December at a suitable time there is a special Mass for the children. A local artist has made two large life-size, cut-out figures. One is of Saint Nicholas in his Bishop's robes and the other of Father Christmas in his traditional attire. An effort has been made to point out the similarity between the white-trimmed red tunic of Santa Claus and the episcopal robes of the Saint-Bishop. After the reading of the Gospel the celebrant recounts the story of the three young ladies and the bags of gold. The priest then calls the children up to receive a gift of a little bag of gold foil-covered chocolate coins, with a little word to each, along the lines of, 'Show your love in always sharing what you have.'

If it is not possible for such a service to take place in

either the parish church or the school, it can form part of the family preparations for Christmas. The parents or parent can gather the children together and tell the story, afterwards presenting the little bags of 'coins' with suitable words.

Toy Service

The parish, home and school come together at the annual school nativity play. They may also combine for a toy service, which involves caring for the wider neighbourhood. It is good for the children to think of Christmas as a time for giving – when God so loved us that He gave His son – and not just receiving. They too must learn to give. A parish (or school) toy service presents just such an opportunity.

The parish's principal Mass on the third Sunday of Advent is a very suitable time with the joyful theme of the readings. Care with the liturgy and preparation of the music can mean a greater involvement of the children. The school can help in the preparations – Bidding prayers and readings looked after by the older children and perhaps with the involvement of the school choir. The school can also remind the children to bring a toy – not a broken cast-off but a new or good used one. The emphasis, it must be remembered, is not upon the toys being given but upon the needy children of the neighbourhood who will benefit from them. After the Gospel, as the first part of the offertory procession, the children can bring up their gifts and the priest can accept these before the altar. The altar servers may stack them round the base of the altar or on the altar steps. If it is possible, a representative from the local social services can be invited to attend and offered the opportunity, at the end of the service, to accept the toys on behalf of the local families in need and to say a 'thank you' to all the children for their kindness and generosity.

Fairies or Angels

'I'm going to be a fairy.' How many five or six-year-olds, over the years, have come home from school in the weeks before Christmas and announced their forthcoming appearance in the school nativity play with these words? Most young children understandably get mixed up over angels and fairies. Some get it sorted out quite well – 'Angels help God and fairies help Father Christmas!'

The rich imaginary world of the young child is not harmed by a belief in fairies any more than Father Christmas, but adults should help them to understand that angels are distinct and different. It is yet another opportunity to speak of Jesus and his words, this time about his love for children and the guardian angel Jesus said each child has. 'See that you never despise any of these little ones, for I tell you that their angels in heaven are continually in the presence of my Father in heaven' (Matt. 18:10). All parents would do well to think about the few verses in Matthew's Gospel that come just before that short passage. They stress the importance of setting a good example to our children. To fail them in love, by not giving them time and putting 'obstacles' in their path, is to choose for ourselves a timeless existence apart from He who is love.

Chapter Two

Christmas and Epiphany

THE SHOWING OF LOVE

The three simple words 'I love you' are probably responsible for more joy and sorrow than any other expression. It can be sincerely spoken and mean quite literally what it says or it can be a way to 'use' another person for extreme selfishness. We all know that it is not enough for a husband or wife to say, 'I love you'; they must show it, not on a grand 'with-flowers' occasion, but daily in little actions of help and support. We have already spoken of giving time to our children as a genuine token of our love. Giving time to God too is an indication of our desire to return his love. Giving time to another person is the most valuable expression of love because it's a giving of ourselves and of what is most precious to us.

The Bible says, 'Yes, God loved the world so much that He gave His only Son' (John 3:16). The Father's love for us was so great that He gave that which was most precious to Him; He sent His son into our time-world.

THE ARRIVAL OF A NEW BABY

The birth of a new baby is an exciting time in a family. With understandable pride the parents show off the sign of their love for one another to family, friends and neighbours who flock round to the hospital or home with useful gifts of clothes or baby accessories.

The arrival of a first baby is extra special. The genuine joy and expressions of love from everyone around the couple make the occasion unique in all human experience. Suddenly the pregnancy period, which seems drawn out and never without a little anxiety, is over – there's new life and lots of joy.

Christmas is surely the most popular of the Christian festivals because it is a celebration of 'love' and so intimately touches a deep human need. However much glitter and noise surrounds the festival, deep down it's all about love. At the divine level, God shows His love by giving His son. At the human level, a young couple's first baby is born and, having no family close-by, they show off their child, first to shepherds and then to the Magi (or Kings). (Luke and Matthew in their versions of the story point to the future role of the baby through these 'showings' – for he was to become the Good Shepherd and King of Kings.)

Everything to do with Christmas is about showing love, not as the secular and commercial world would have us believe, about having a good time. The crib in home, school and church shows off the baby – the sign of God's love. The cards we send, the gifts we give, show our love for one another. Even the Christmas tree and decorations show our joy that God so loved the world that He gave us His most precious gift.

CHRISTMAS DECORATIONS

Young children love drawing, colouring and cutting out. The preparations for Christmas provide a wonderful opportunity to use their talents and enthusiasm. Individual cards that are lovingly made, no matter how simply, are much more in keeping with the real spirit of the festival than mass-market shop-bought cards. The same goes for decorations. What does it matter if they aren't as shiny and glittery as those everyone else has. They are expressions of love and should receive pride of place.

There is an obvious tension between the Christmas of the shops, the secular pagan event, and the Christmas of the Church, the celebration of the Incarnation. The first seems to begin earlier and earlier every year – about the third or fourth week of October. It finishes at closing time on 24th December. The religious celebrations begin on the evening of 24th December and extend to 6th January.

The secular Christmas puts a great deal of pressure upon Christian families to conform, to anticipate the celebrations. Up go the home decorations in our neighbours' homes in the first week or two of December and the children begin a bombardment of 'It's not fair, why can't we have our decorations up yet?' This ought to be resisted until the last possible moment, although it may not be possible to hang on until Christmas Eve. When Advent ends, when we pour ourselves into celebration. To anticipate the occasion too much and too soon is to spoil it.

The decorations and the crib, to maintain peace in the family, can go up gradually over a period of days, perhaps during the last week, leaving the crib until last. Some parents may feel, 'Oh, don't be a spoil-sport, let the children have the tree and decorations when they want them. Christmas is for children after all.' Wrong! The key-note of the 'coming' period before Christmas is the *waiting* involved in the long years before the Saviour's birth, the air of expectancy that built up as the Jews waited for their Messiah to come and deliver them. As we use an Advent calendar, wreath, etc. and pray that Christ may come, an atmosphere of expectancy is built up in the family. This can so easily be destroyed or made meaningless if the full 'works' of tree, decorations, crib and so on announce the celebration has come, when we are still in the 'coming' period.

THE CHRISTMAS CRIB

Every family has its own way of arranging their crib. If possible it should be given a very prominent position where visitors to the family will see and benefit from it. St Francis of Assisi's original crib used living animals and real people. It was intended to teach; so should ours. It must not become an automatic feature of the decorations, put up with little care and thought in the same idle way it has always been erected. There's no better way than to make the children responsible for it, finding, if possible, real straw to put in it, drawing and colouring a new background, arranging the figures, etc.

Ideally the crib should not be put up until Christmas Eve or at least a couple of days before Christmas. It's rather a nice idea not to add the figure of the baby until just before or just after Midnight Mass. If none of the family are going to the Midnight Mass, the figure can be added late on Christmas Eve. Some families make a little ceremony out of this. The front of the prepared stable is covered, with the other figures arranged inside. The children go upstairs (or wherever they have kept the 'baby' ready for this occasion) and bring it into the room singing 'Away in a manger' or any carol of their choice. If there are responsible older children available they might lead a little procession with one or two lighted candles. (These could be borrowed for the occasion from the Advent wreath.) When the family is gathered round the crib, the head of the family might like to read a simple blessing.

'Bless, Almighty Father, this crib which we have (made) prepared to remind us of the birth, long ago, of your beloved Son. His coming brought light and hope to the world. May our lives be lit up with our love of Jesus, who lives in our hearts by faith.'

It is very important that the figures of the Magi (the three Kings) are not put in or near the crib yet. They will be added later, on the feast of Epiphany.

CHRISTMAS GIFTS

The name 'Christmas' comes from the old English words 'Cristes Maesse' or Christ's Mass, emphasising what has always been the highlight of the festival for the Catholic family. Mass together as a family, whether this is at midnight or in the morning, is the special occasion we have been building up to during the weeks of Advent. In and through the Mass each family group, forming the parish family, unites in offering to the Father the gift of love that He cannot refuse. In return He gives us in Holy

Communion, our Christmas gift – His Son, as our spiritual nourishment and strength.

Each family has its own tradition of how and when to exchange Christmas gifts. Ideally this should be linked in some way with the gift we receive from God the Father. The sacramental gift of Jesus, the risen Christ, on the very day we recall how God so loved the world that He gave us His Son, is *the* Christmas moment. All else afterwards merely celebrates this. And the first thing we can do, if possible, is to exchange our personal gifts.

CELEBRATING A BIRTHDAY

One of the earliest songs a toddler learns is 'Happy Birthday to you . . .' As this comes so naturally to them, they can be encouraged to sing it on Christmas Day around the crib. It lays the foundation for a more adult understanding later on.

There may be the opportunity, excitement permitting, to discuss with older children and teenagers what we are doing when we celebrate a birthday. They can easily grasp that a birthday celebrates the gift of life, given on a precise day at a particular moment in time. But it is not the day of the year we are happy about, but the gift of life itself. This is obvious when we think about parents' birthdays. Most children are not very sure how old their mother or father is, and very few would know on what day of the week or at what time of day their mum or dad was born. So a birthday card and present has got nothing to do with the *day* or the *time* of the birth, rather it says, 'we love you and we are grateful for your being here.' It is a celebration of life: that's why, of course, we do not celebrate the birthdays of dead members of our families.

In celebrating the birthday of Jesus every year we are not interested in the time of day, or the day, or year (which no one knows for certain). We are rejoicing that Jesus, the

Son of God, was born as one of us and is still alive and with us. The 'once-upon-a-time' of the inhabited crib (one cave) only has any meaning through our faith in the empty tomb (the second cave). If we did not believe that Jesus was now alive and with us, there would never have been any such event as Christmas. And this is why Easter is more important than Christmas.

THE TWELVE DAYS OF CHRISTMAS

For the Christian family 'Christmas' continues until 6th January. Although Dad goes back to work and the children may even return to school the Christmas season is not closed until after the celebration of Epiphany. So the decorations should not come down until the 'wise men' have had a chance to get to the crib! Everyone would agree that these three traditional figures play an important part in the Christmas scenario, but so often they get little or no part of the celebrations.

In the early years of the Church, when eventually Christ's birth day was celebrated – which didn't happen for the first 250 years – the Eastern Christians kept it on 6th January and in the West the Church celebrated on 25th December. Of course this caused some confusion! It was resolved in the end by the Western Church extending their celebrations to 6th January which became the feast of 'the showing' or manifestation which is the meaning of the word 'Epiphany'. So we now have the famous 'twelve days of Christmas', from 25th December to 6th January.

FEAST OF THE FAMILY

'Last year we went to your Mum's on Christmas Day and my family's on Boxing Day . . . I think we ought to visit my parents this Christmas . . we can go on to your Mum and Dad's on Boxing day.'

'No, if we do that we'll . . .'

Every year many families have the problem of who is going where and when over Christmas. A great effort is made to get together and not miss anyone out over the holiday period. To be together, to show love for these three or four days in the year is important. No matter how much has been spent on Christmas gifts, it's the giving, in person if possible, which really matters. Love is no better expressed than in giving. It's at this time that the description of the family by Pope John Paul II, as 'the community of love' really rings true.

The Church very wisely takes advantage of all this by emphasising the importance and value of the family. It places the feast of the Holy Family on 30th December. The point of this is not just to remind us that the individual members of that special family were all 'holy', but that the way to holiness for the great majority of us is through the family. 'Christian marriage is the pathway to holiness for all members of the family' (Pope John Paul II at York).

We have to help our children (and ourselves too, for that matter) to an understanding that 'holiness' does not mean 'odd', 'peculiar' or 'abnormal'. For this reason, that which was ordinary and quite normal about the Holy Family must always be stressed with children. Most pictures of the Holy Family don't help and should be avoided! At best they are 'twee' and at worst are so misleading as to present, in the long term, possible danger to the child's faith.

A word or two of explanation: Certainly we believe that Jesus is, and will always be, the Son of God. But that *belief* that we have can under-value, or perhaps even destroy our like belief that he was a normal human being as well; like us in *all* things, Paul reminded us, except he could not sin. Little boys can do lots of naughty things that are not 'sins'. Untidiness is not a sin, a dirty face is not sinful, and so on. If in later life the man Jesus was so obviously normal and ordinary-looking that his closest friends took a long time, and indeed found it difficult to say, 'You are the Messiah,' he must have looked and behaved very like any other village lad in Nazareth. So the Holy Family was just like ours – with only one difference – there was no deliberate offence given to God. That leaves plenty of room for Mary and Joseph to struggle with their impatience when Jesus was naughty; for Joseph to be worried sick about where his next bit of work was coming from; for Mary to be subjected to the latest piece of gossip over the garden wall. That the boy Jesus could cause worry can be seen from the only glimpse of life in the Holy Family we get, when at the age of twelve he was lost in Jerusalem.

The best way to note the feast day in the family, besides a special grace at meal times (see page 67) is to discuss and bring out the humanness of this special family. Mothers, in their own prayers, can and should ask Mary, as an understanding mother, to help with her prayers. Fathers too should not hesitate to ask Joseph for some assistance when housing causes headaches, money is scarce, or redundancy threatens.

EPIPHANY – THE SHOWING

Surprisingly the feast of Epiphany is older than Christmas itself, being kept in the Eastern part of the Roman Empire from the very earliest times. It still remains a more important day than the 25th December for most Eastern Christians. This is probably because they have retained a better understanding of what the feast means. This is the showing of the infant Jesus to the non-Jewish Magi, emphasising that the Christian faith was to be for all, not just for the Jews.

There are a few simple ceremonies that can help the family mark this special day. The Magi, or kings, were not put in the crib (see page 37) on Christmas Eve. Some families have the lovely little custom of making them journey to the crib from a starting point somewhere in the house.

This need not be in the same room and they can begin the journey any time after 25th December. Moved a little way each day but timed to arrive, after the hazards of their journey across furniture and perhaps floor space, at the crib on 6th January. With the aid of Blu-Tack a star can travel a little ahead of them. The shepherds, of course, will have been removed long before they arrive to make room for the Magi so that it's clearly their special day.

DRESSING UP

Young children, especially girls, love dressing up and this is the best feast day in the year for that. The event is tailor-made for dressing up and playing out the story. It's important to remember that although *tradition* says there were *three* wise men or kings, the Gospel of Matthew (which is the only one to tell the story) does not say how many there were. It merely says, 'Some wise men came from the East.' Now this is very useful to remember if there are insufficient children for three 'kings', so two children can dress up and bring the three gifts or if there are numerous children there can be more than three kings; naturally these 'kings' will need attendants, not to mention camels, donkeys and so on.

Making crowns and gifts and dressing up will take best part of an afternoon. The gifts could be specially made for the occasion or household ornaments, i.e. jewellery cases or musical boxes could (with permission) be commandeered. The 'journey' or procession from a bedroom to the crib can be made into a splendid affair. After the presentation of the presents at the crib there is a wonderful opportunity for a little surprise party (Mum or Dad can prepare this secretly to make the occasion the chance for a special treat). A simple 'crown' cake or sponge-cake could be baked in the rough shape of a crown with encrusted small colourful sweets as jewels. Presented just after the 'gold', 'frankincense' and 'myrrh', the little party will not only round off the celebration perfectly but will also help the children to appreciate that Christian festivals can be fun.

EPIPHANY BLESSING

Since very early times tradition has had it that there were three visitors to the infant Jesus. This probably arose because three gifts were brought. They were usually thought of as kings too, possibly because of Psalm seventy-two which says, 'The kings of Tarshish and of the islands will pay him tribute. The kings of Sheba and Seba will offer gifts . . .' At some time in the remote and distant past they were given the names of Caspar, Melchior and Baltassar.

In some countries, where the greater number of the population are Catholic, for example Poland, there is a very ancient tradition of a special blessing for the home at Epiphany-time. The blessing is closely associated with Caspar, Melchior and Baltassar. After the blessing of the home they chalk up C + M + B, and add the year, over the doorway. While it could be an opportunity to invite the parish priest or his assistant to come and bless the house, the head of the household, of course, could ask a blessing on the house.

THE BAPTISM OF JESUS

After thinking about babies and families for so long it comes as something of a shock on the very first Sunday after the Epiphany to find the Church wanting us to consider the baptism of Our Lord – at the age of thirty! Naturally being a Jewish little boy Jesus was named at his circumcision, a few days after his birth. It is his public work as a preacher that begins with his baptism by his cousin John. His circumcision was a quiet family affair involving only his immediate family but his baptism, when he took up his preaching work, was a public act – a showing to the world.

When we thought about the 'coming' season before Christmas we discovered that the Church wants us to realise that there are three comings of Christ (see page 20). At Christmas time too we are helped to see that there was more than one 'showing' of Jesus. As a new-born baby he was shown first to the shepherds (he would become the Good Shepherd), some time later he was shown to the Magi, or kings (he would be the 'king of kings') and now, as a man, he is marked out among the crowds.

You will remember what happened: Jesus, trying to find out what his Father wanted him to do, went up from his home at Nazareth to the place on the banks of the Jordan where his cousin John was preaching and baptising. There Jesus asked to be baptised and as he came up out of the water a voice spoke from heaven: 'This is my Son, the Beloved; my favour rests on him' (Matthew 3:17).

Jesus, of course, would have been 'ducked-under' by John in the waters of the river Jordan. While the Catholic Church no longer baptises in this way, by total immersion, it was the method of the early Church.

This picture shows a kind of font or baptistery that was used by the Church in the first two or three hundred years of its existence. This drawing is based on a font preserved in a museum in Carthage, North Africa.

It was used in this way: The adult wanting to join the Christian community showed his faith and love for Christ by passing through the waters of baptism to a new life.

The priest would stand at point P, the catechumen (the adult convert) at point C and a Deacon at point D. After making his act of faith the catechumen would step down into the water in the centre (it was probably lapping over his feet where he was standing at C). The priest would help him to submerge in the water while he, the priest, said the words of the sacrament, 'I baptise you in the name of the Father and of the Son and of the Holy Spirit.' As the new Christian emerged from the water the deacon would wrap a white baptismal robe round him.

He may well have been presented at the same time with a lighted candle, a symbol of his new role as light-bearer, to follow after Christ, 'the light of the world', and take Christ's light out to the world. You can see how, with this method of baptising, the new Christian passed *through* the waters of baptism as well as going *under* the waters. He also achieved this by and through the cross. It was in this way that the early Church kept Paul's words in mind: 'When we were baptised we went into the tomb with him and joined him in death, so that as Christ was raised from the dead by the Father's glory, we too might live a new life' (Rom. 6:4).

For an adult of that time turning formally away from paganism, the acceptance of baptism was a very solemn and life-changing act. It was the most dramatic and important step they would ever take. That complete commitment and gift of self to Christ could, and in thousands of cases did, result in torture and death. (Yet so many people accepted the challenge of baptism that within three hundred years the work of that little band of twelve Apostles had grown to the virtual conversion of the Roman world.) Those who escaped martyrdom must have lived out their lives of commitment and been real 'lights' to the world.

However hard we, today, try to make the baptism of a baby full of meaning and purpose, it lacks the dramatic impact originally experienced. Most of us were baptised as children and of course haven't the faintest memory of the most important religious act in our life. That is why parents must not lightly ask for baptism for their child and must look for every possible means to prepare themselves and the godparents well for the sacrament.

In recent years a great effort has been made in most parishes to help adult Catholics come to a better knowledge and appreciation of their Faith. This usually takes the form of an occasional course or series of talks. Faced with children's needs and questioning parents will realise their own need for a more mature grasp of the Faith. Opportunities to put this right should be seized and used.

Because parents act on behalf of their child in saying, 'This is what we ask for our child,' they must, as the child grows up, help them to understand what has happened. This in practice means, among other things, not missing an opportunity to recall and celebrate the anniversary of the child's baptism. (See page 118.) The feast of Christ's baptism is one such opportunity when the child's baptismal candle can be got out and, using it as a table centrepiece at Sunday dinner, lit for a few minutes with a word or two of explanation.

Gifts that a child receives on his or her christening day usually disappear into cupboards and drawers. As a continual reminder of that important day, if the gifts are suitable for this, a special shelf in a wall unit, bookcase or sideboard could be set aside for the gifts to be put on show. The baptismal candle and certificate perhaps can be given pride of place. Such a shelf is a continual reminder to the whole family of the importance of baptism.

Christmas is a time for the family. It is the time when we recall the Holy Family and immediately afterwards we are reminded that as Christians we are adopted members of God's family – sons and daughters of God through our baptism.

SHOWING LOVE TO OTHER MEMBERS OF THE CHRISTIAN FAMILY

It cannot be a coincidence that the week of prayer for Christian unity follows so soon after Christmas, from 18th January to 25th. This week should not pass the family by unnoticed.

As family life is the setting in which children grow to understand and share love, it's there too that they learn what unity is. There is no better place for an understanding love of other Christians to grow and be nurtured.

Some families, of course, are inter-Church but many more consist of a Catholic and a partner who is not committed to any particular Church. In both of these cases the family has an opportunity to talk and pray about Church differences. Of course there has got to be a lot of sensitivity on the Catholic partner's side not to make a non-Catholic partner feel 'got at' or 'put on the spot'. Nor should impertinent questions be tolerated from the younger members of the family; at all times an individual's freedom of choice and personal decision should be respected. In chatting with young people the responsible free choice adults have should be made clear.

The local parish priest will have received copies of the prayer leaflet issued by the British Council of Churches. Mum or Dad could ask for a copy very soon after Christmas. It will give a list of prayer intentions for use over the eight days. However, not all of the leaflet will be helpful for family prayer but it should, at the very least, stimulate a mention of some aspect or other of Christian unity during the week. It's better to limit the intentions, keeping them local and practical; praying, for example, for the people in our town (village, borough, etc.) that go to the Methodist church, or the Salvation Army hall etc. There's sure to be a local united service and the family ought to try and send at least one representative.

Learning how to show love is the family's work and showing love to our brothers and sisters in the wider Christian family should be very high on our list of priorities.

THE OFFERING OF LOVE

Two-year-old Sharon and her friend Michael, who was nearly four, were playing happily in the garden. Suddenly their mums, who were enjoying a quiet cup of coffee in the kitchen, were disturbed by a great commotion. Rushing to the window they saw both children trying to jam themselves, at the same time, on the seat of the one and only small tricycle. After much shouting and screeching both managed to squeeze on, but neither could move! When their mums got to them Sharon was sobbing and Michael was stoutly and loudly proclaiming, 'If one of us got off *I* could ride it properly.'

It was resolved that they would take turns. Michael had the first short ride up the concrete garden path, pursued after less than thirty seconds by Sharon, calling, 'Me turn, me turn.'

Experienced parents will recognise that as an ordinary everyday sort of story from any place where children play together. 'Me-me-me' is a regularly heard cry and the attitude underlying all the play of very young children. When the youngster follows his natural desire to eat with his fingers, drops food all over the floor or squats on the carpet behind the settee instead of on the potty, a parent realises how close the young human is to the animal kingdom! This closeness shows particularly in the instinctive drive for self-preservation; for example, taking hand-fuls of biscuits instead of the one expected. The 'me-me-me' and the strong natural self-love it shows is the self-preservation instinct in full swing.

LEARNING UNSELFISH LOVE

One of parents' most important tasks is to develop in their children an awareness and love of others – quite simply to teach them to share. This is something that has to be *learnt*, just as the child has to learn how to use a knife and fork or the toilet. No one *naturally* puts others first, before him or herself.

That natural and necessary strong self-love that we are each born with has to be broadened out, channelled and developed. While retaining a healthy self-love (so that we look after ourselves properly and avoid danger), in-growing love has to be turned out to others. The child learns to share by the way family life is organised and run – does dad do a share of the washing-up? – and prin-cipally by example. In play too, the child learns to take turns and let others have a go.

The learning goes on all through life. There is no cut-off point because we are all, to a greater or lesser degree, selfish people. The really mature person is the one who is most unselfish, who has the greatest love and considera-tion for others. Our daily newspapers sometimes carry stories of heroic unselfishness:

'Wife throws herself in front of husband as terrorist fires.'
'Scout leader shields youngster from falling rocks with his own body.'

Some other people live heroically unselfish lives hardly noticed by the world, as patiently and lovingly, year in and year out, they care for a very demanding physically or mentally handicapped child.

Jesus summed all this up when he said, 'No greater love can a man have than to give his life for another.'

Love compels action; the wife did not stop to think – should she or shouldn't she shield her husband – nor did the scout leader. A 'me-me-me' person would not have acted! Only years of generous self-giving could prompt such an immediate offering of oneself.

GROWTH TO MATURITY

True Christian maturity has got –
   – nothing to do with being physically big and strong or good or bad looking.
   – nothing to do with being well-educated with exam passes and degrees.
   – nothing to do with being black or white, this nationality or that.
But it has everything to do with struggling daily with self-love and developing an outward-going love of others.

We are reminded, yet again, of Paul's words:

'If I have all the eloquence of men or of angels, but speak without love, I am simply a gong booming or a cymbal clashing. If I have the gift of prophecy, understanding all the mysteries there are, and knowing everything, and if I have faith in all its fulness, to move mountains, but without love, then I am nothing at all' (I Cor. 13).

So there is only one road to maturity and that is the road of self-discipline. This means working with God's grace to turn an in-growing love outwards, or more simply saying 'no' more often to ourselves and 'yes' to others.

Family life is not easy! Nor is learning self-discipline.

Parents have to be learning it as, at the same time, they are guiding their children. In fact the very living-out of daily family life is a discipline for parents. The good mum runs around at the beck and call of the family when she would love to sit quiet for a few minutes; the good dad will play with the children and read to them before becoming engrossed in sport on TV.

Children can only learn self-discipline by learning to obey in the home. A youngster will never learn to say 'no' to himself later in life if he hasn't learnt to respond to the 'no' said to him in the family. An obedience based on love is all-important. This is the sort of obedience Jesus expects of his followers.

'If you love me,' he says, 'you will do what I ask'
(Jn 15:10)
And what does he ask?
'You must love your neighbour as yourself'
(Matt. 19:19).
Failing to do that is to sin. To deliberately turn love, which should be given to 'Love' itself, in on ourselves is to offend God.

THE SEASON OF LENT

Lent is the season offered to us by the Church when we can make a special effort with self-discipline. It is *offered* to us because we can quite easily sail through Lent without using the opportunity. But if we do that we and our family are the losers. We will receive encouragement but no one will check up if we respond or not.

Named after the old English word 'lenten' which means 'spring', the season was first intended as a preparation period for the new converts who were getting ready for baptism. In the early years of Christianity this took place at the Easter vigil. Later the season was applied to all Christians and their need for an annual effort to renew themselves. Christians who had sinned seriously and now wanted to return to the active life of the community were prepared throughout these forty days for reconciliation at Easter. As a sign of their sorrow they wore clothes of sacking and ashes were sprinkled on their heads. By the ninth century this custom had stopped and was replaced by a ceremony involving the whole Church. To remind the whole community that each and every one was a sinner, ashes were placed on their heads on the first day of Lent. As this took place on a Wednesday the day naturally became Ash Wednesday.

TO EASTER THROUGH LENT

Only Easter makes sense of Lent. Only the Resurrection makes sense of Christ's birth, life and death. Jesus's death, on its own, was not special. He offered himself to his Father on the cross, but if the Father had not accepted his offering that would have been the end of it. However, the Father did show his acceptance by raising His Son up to a new life. Easter is, for that reason, the most important festival in the Church's year, the celebration of the main event of God's work in the world.

Given the great fuss that is made of Christmas it isn't surprising that most people fail to appreciate the importance of Easter. Children find it particularly difficult to take in. All those lovely presents, decorations and parties are in strong contrast to what happens at Easter! A few chocolate Easter Eggs doesn't right the balance! In the family a great effort needs to be made to give the celebration of Easter a proper emphasis and dignity. And this isn't possible without taking the forty days of Lent seriously.

What we have got to absorb and gradually impart to our family is the message of Lent. This is, as we have been saying, that we must die to our own selfishness so that we can rise up joyfully with Christ to a new life.

It is *a time for* – *a change of heart*. A time for a new and closer look at the way our lives are lived, for repentance and reconciliation.

It is *a time for* – *concern for others*. Caring for others is a valuable weapon in our fight against selfishness. Almsgiving has always been a part of Lent.

It is *a time for* – *prayer which costs*. That means in terms of time and personal effort.

When any 'giving-up' or mortification is spoken of at the outset of Lent these three things must be kept in mind – our need for a change of heart, an outward and genuine concern for others and, underlying everything, a need to pray much more.

Each of these three parts to Lent must be present if the season is to have any real and lasting value. To go into Lent with a resolution to give up sugar in our tea, for example, is only of any value if it is part of our 'change of heart' campaign. The money saved should go to our deprived brothers and sisters and the action supported by an increased effort at prayer.

ASH WEDNESDAY

From the word go at breakfast on Ash Wednesday morning the family needs to understand that the next few weeks point us to the celebration of Christ's resurrection. Grace before meals (see page 67) that day can keep Easter in mind from the beginning.

For children actions speak louder than words so attendance at the Mass of the ashes is important. The simple dramatic symbolism can mark very clearly the specialness of this time. Seeing who has still got his ashes showing at the evening meal time can lead naturally into some talk about the meaning of the ashes and so on to the purpose of Lent.

FAMILY SERVICE OF THE ASHES

If the family cannot get to a Mass at which the ashes are blessed and bestowed then a little evening ceremony in the home is easily arranged. The proper thing is to make the ashes from the palms given the previous year on Palm Sunday. Many families keep their blessed palms but if you haven't done so another piece of unblessed (dry) ever-green would do. (Always save your palms from one year to the next just in case you need them.) If one or two members of the family have already received the ashes there is no reason why they cannot take part in a private family celebration.

Just before or after the evening meal is a good time. It could be a kind of extended 'grace' or 'table prayer'. A couple of the small individual palms can be cut up into short pieces and burnt carefully in a small basin or saucer. The head of the household can read a prayer of blessing over them. A prayer similar to the following might be suitable –

Let us ask our heavenly Father to bless these ashes which we will use as a mark of our repentance.
(pause)
Lord, bless these ashes.
Wearing them reminds us that we are from the dust of the earth.
Pardon our sins and keep us faithful to the resolutions we have made for Lent.
Help us to prepare well for the celebration of Your Son's glorious resurrection.
This we ask through the same Jesus Christ.   Amen.

Then dipping his thumb in the ashes, he marks each forehead with the words –

'Turn away from sin and be faithful to the Gospel.'

The simple ceremony can close with this prayer –

Loving Father, today we start Lent.
Over the next six weeks, with your help, we are going to prepare for Easter.
From today we are making a new start with a bigger effort to be more loving and kind.
Help us to show concern for the less fortunate, the hungry and the poor,
and especially help us to speak to you more often.
We ask this through Your Son, Jesus,
whose death and resurrection we will be thinking about in the next few weeks.

Amen.

Younger members of the family may well get a fit of the giggles. If they do, allow it to take its course without over-reacting. This is no reason for abandoning or not trying the ceremony. Simple action-signs repeated year after year have a lasting impact.

RESOLUTIONS FOR LENT

A faithful and sincere living of the Christian life means a continual effort to live up to the ideals Christ has set us. Because we so regularly fall short we are constantly picking ourselves up and making a new effort, a new beginning.

Lent is a terrific opportunity to make such a fresh start. This in effect means making resolutions. They should be few, practical and reasonable. A little self-knowledge should be brought to bear. It's quite pointless making great promises to go, for example, to daily Mass if you know yourself well enough to know you won't keep it up. However you might reasonably organise yourself to get to Mass once or twice in the week.

Besides the above there is only one golden rule about Lenten resolutions. Never give up or take on anything which will have an adverse effect upon the family. The classic example is smoking – if dad's resolution to give up smoking makes him like a bear with a sore head and a 'pain' to live with, he mustn't do it, at least not during Lent. On the other hand dad or mum's smoking may already be very unpleasant – and unhealthy – for the rest of the family. Then one might give up smoking as a mark of love and respect for those who share the same home.

Having a change of heart does not mean being miserable or making others suffer. If mum's resolution to help with the Church cleaning during Lent takes her away from her own cleaning and household duties or means the house is empty when the children come home from school, then she should find something else to do.

Nothing that is done supposedly for the love of God which interferes with our love and responsibility to the family may ever be undertaken. Our first duty is to love God through the loving service we give to our family.

PREPARING FOR RECONCILIATION

Selfishness and self-love is the enemy we are out to deal a blow to during Lent. We should try and see our resolutions and Lenten efforts as a preparation for the sacrament of reconciliation (confession).

Going to confession is not something we 'fit in' in order to fulfil a duty just before Easter. Receiving the ashes at the start of Lent should be seen as the start of our six weeks of preparation for receiving the sacrament in Holy Week.

In most parishes the children of seven-plus make their first confession during this traditional period of sorrow for sin. This is a time of special co-operation between school, parish and home – the triangle of educational and pastoral care. What goes on in the classroom may well set the pace but the parish and home should be equally involved. Local ways of proceeding vary from place to place but everywhere it is agreed that the whole family should be involved in some way in the preparation.

This is a most important time for the 7–8-year-olds. They did not choose to be baptised nor, of course, do they remember it. This is therefore their first public religious act. On no account should a child be forced, pressurised or bribed into receiving the sacrament – or going to Holy Communion – for the first time. There is no loss in leaving it another year or two. What other people, including teachers and clergy, may say or think must be regarded purely as advice. The parent has the final decision. If the child is clearly not ready or is unwilling, on no account must he or she be talked into it. To do so may well set up a chain reaction and sow the seeds of a total rejection of the Faith in the teens.

The willing child should be helped to see that going to the sacraments for the first time is an important step towards becoming a grown-up Christian. It is a kind of first sign of a 'coming of age', because now they will be bound, as are adults, to go to Mass on Sundays and Holy Days.

FRIDAYS OF LENT

The final few days of Lent are the climax of these six weeks, and the most important of these days is Good Friday. In fact it's that day which casts its long shadow over the preceding weeks. All our efforts at self-discipline – saying 'no' to ourselves – are only of any real value if they are linked to Christ's love and obedience that took him to the cross. It is his obedient love that wins for us the forgiveness of the Father. And He will bless our efforts and raise us up if all that we do in Lent is offered with and through His obedient Son.

In the Church's calendar each week is thought of as the year in miniature. The highlight of the year is Easter Sunday – the highlight of the week is Sunday when we gather together to recall and celebrate Christ's rising from the dead. Every Friday we are asked to recall the events of Good Friday.

FISH ON FRIDAYS

The 'why' of the old rule about 'fish on Fridays' (really it was abstaining from meat) was not often explained. It had become just one of those odd things that Catholics did. The original intention was that each Friday we should recall that this was the day of the week on which Jesus died. And in recalling this mark it with an act of sorrow for sin.

When the obligation to abstain from meat on a Friday was done away with (not a lot of point when two-thirds of the world *never* see meat to eat) we were asked to carry on doing something of our own choosing. The day still needed to be recalled and we always need to express sorrow for sin. In fact, sadly, very few people ever think about it!

The six (seven including Good Friday) Fridays of Lent

are a little special and – together with Sunday – can be the focal points of the weeks of Lent. One use of the day can be to link the ancient tradition of fasting during Lent with the concern we should have for the deprived. CAFOD (Catholic Fund for Overseas Development) organises one special 'family fast day' in Lent, but there's no good reason why families can't make every Friday a 'family fast day'. By going without one full meal or reducing two of the meals, our own 'no' to ourselves can be a positive 'yes' to the needy.

FRIDAY PRAYER

The 'table prayer' (see page 67) of Lenten Fridays also offers an opportunity to make these days a bit different. At the principal meal of the day when hopefully most of the family are present, an adapted and simplified Way of the Cross can be used. There are two methods of using it. The first way, in a family where the children are quite young, is to spread the seven 'stations' over the seven Fridays of Lent, one each week. The second method, where the family are older, is to use the whole thing, involving if possible each member of the family round the table. You will need to bring your Bible to the table.

WAY OF THE CROSS

[Set out here for use week by week over a period of seven weeks. If it is all to be used at one time ignore the references to First Friday, Second Friday etc.]

First Friday of Lent
  1. *Jesus is condemned to death.* Read: John 19:4–11 and 16. Let us say sorry to God for the times we have

talked unkindly and unjustly about other people (and called them names). Please God help us not to judge others.   Amen.

Second Friday of Lent

2. *Jesus is met by his mother*. Tradition tells us that Jesus met Mary on the Way of the Cross. Certainly Mary's great love would have prompted her to be there. This love-poem from the Bible tells us how she would have felt: 'I sought . . .' from The Song of Songs 3:1–4. Let us say sorry to God for the times we have upset and hurt those we love most. Please God help us to love and respect our family.   Amen.

Third Friday of Lent

3. *The cross is laid upon Simon of Cyrene*. Read: Mark 15:21. Let us say sorry to God for the times when we have not offered to help other people, especially people in real need. Please God help us to give our help generously to anyone who needs it. Amen.

Fourth Friday of Lent

4. *The women of Jerusalem mourn for Our Lord*. Read: Luke 23:27–32. Let us say sorry to God for the times when we have been proud and not admitted that we were in the wrong. Please God help us to be humble and ask forgiveness when we have sinned.   Amen.

Fifth Friday of Lent

5. *Jesus is stripped of his clothes*. Read: John 19:23 and 24. Let us say sorry to God for the times when we have been selfish and pushed ourselves in front of others. Please God help us to strip ourselves of our selfishness.   Amen.

Sixth Friday of Lent

6. *Jesus is nailed to the cross*. Read: Luke 23:33 and 34. Let us say sorry to God for the times when our hands and feet have led us into sin. Please God

help us to be always honest and trustworthy.
Amen.

Seventh Friday of Lent

7. *Jesus dies on the cross*. Read: Matthew 27:45–50. Let us say sorry to God for all the times we have failed in our love for him and not obeyed his wishes. Please God help us to grow in love for you and give you the obedience you look for.   Amen.

THE EASTER TREE

We are very fortunate that in our part of the world the seasonal pattern of nature helps us to a better understanding of the meaning of Lent and Easter. The apparently dead winter trees and bushes are gradually transformed during this period. By Easter Sunday fresh green leaves are showing the rebirth of nature. What was dead, dark and cold is showing life, light and hope. As far as possible, according to where you live, the children's attention needs to be drawn to this annual transformation in Nature. And, of course, a parallel should be drawn with our own lives as Christians.

The Easter tree is one good way of tying the two together. On a large sheet of white card, or on a surface taken from the inside of a large used cereal packet, draw a simple outline of a tree in winter, including the roots. Cut out the outline (don't make the branches and twigs too fussy otherwise there will be problems) leaving the roots in the ground. Get the children to colour the trunk and branches brown – nothing more, because it is representing an apparently dead tree in winter. Mount the tree on a second piece of card allowing about a quarter of an inch (or a centimetre) between the two cards. Write the heading above the tree on the backing card: Easter Tree. On Ash Wednesday hang the Easter Tree in your kitchen where everyone can see it. On that day get the children to make a sheet (possibly one each) of little ovals which they colour green. These are to be the leaves and their dimension should be kept in some sort of proportion with the tree.

The tree works in relationship with the resolutions (see page 57) that have been made by the family for Lent. Each time (perhaps once a day so that they can all be done together) a good turn has been done etc., a green leaf is stuck onto the tree. By the time Easter Sunday comes the tree should be covered in foliage. The roots, which should not have been coloured brown when the trunk was, can be coloured in for each of the Sunday Masses and holy communions of Lent: it is from our Sunday worship together and the reception of the risen Christ in holy communion, that the grace and strength comes to live our lives as children of God. It is from union with Christ and his community that we receive the grace and strength to do good actions.

On Easter Day the tree will serve as a decoration and lovely memorial of our efforts throughout Lent. On Easter morning, to symbolise the resurrection, little yellow or white bows can be tied between the green leaves around the branches.

PRAYER IN THE FAMILY

A lot of parents feel that they would like their family to pray together but, not knowing how to get started or because they feel embarrassed to suggest it, never get round to it. The beginning of Lent provides the perfect opportunity to make a start. And making a resolute start is half the battle: the other half consists in trying to remember to do it every day, keeping it simple and trying to make it enjoyable. Before we look at each of those points in turn there are a few background thoughts to keep in mind.

Background

'Ann looks more like her mother every day.'

'Richard's mad keen on sport like his Dad.'

We can't help our children growing up looking a bit like us, with some of our mannerisms, habits and interests. It's sure to happen because from their very earliest moments they have watched us closely and have imitated us.

When we start talking about prayer we must not forget that prayer cannot be *taught*, it has to be *caught*. If mum and dad do not see the real point of praying and only 'go through the motions' then children will know immediately. It is a total waste of time for parents to send young children off to bed with a 'don't forget your prayers' then turn their immediate attention back to their favourite TV show. Children will only learn to pray (this is different from learning to say a prayer, see page 71) if they see their parents praying.

The first point to make, then, is that if you want your family to pray *you* must pray and be seen to pray. This is sure to mean sacrificing yourself a little – not sinking into the newspaper so quickly in the evening for instance, or perhaps missing some viewing time.

From the beginning it's a good idea for the parents to keep the target or goal in mind: to get the family – over a period of time – so 'at home' with prayer that it becomes 'natural' for them to pray easily anywhere, at any time, about any and everything.

'A resolute start'

The younger the children the easier it is to start. Most teenagers get embarrassed about praying with the family (they're frightened their friends will find out and they will be made to look silly in front of them) but this should not stand in the way of the rest of the family going ahead. Many a conscientious objector secretly wants to take part in spite of himself (or herself) and later will find it possible to join in. No child is too young to be included and often it's the youngest who will remind the others that it's time to talk to God!

Having made up your mind, fix a definite starting time; for example, the evening meal of Ash Wednesday when all the family might be together. There is no better way to start than with grace before meals. This wonderful old custom has largely fallen into disuse. This may be because meals have become, in so many families, fragmented things. For example: Paul eating now, because he's got to rush off to football practice; Clare, a little later because she couldn't be enticed away from the TV any sooner; Dad a bit later still because his train was late getting in and so on.

Meal-times should be focal points of the day, when the family (or as much of it as possible) are together, sharing the same table, the same food and the conversation. Every effort should be made to keep the family united in this (see page 90); there is a lot more at stake – in the long term – than a football practice, or a TV story. So often one hears of a family that has fallen apart because the various members have not communicated with one another. They have each gone their own way, strangers to one another in the same building. As soon as the first child can sit in a high chair the family tradition of always eating together – unless really impossible – should be laid down.

Grace before meals is a good place to start family prayer because it is generally a recognised and understood prayer with which people are familiar. Use a simple prayer to begin with, perhaps the traditional one, 'Bless us, O Lord, and these thy gifts which we are about to receive from Thy bounty', or one of the following short prayers, or possibly one the children use at school; this will get over the natural awkwardness of a new experience.

Try one of these –

> Come, Lord Jesus, be our guest,
> And may our meal by you be blest.   Amen.

Great God and giver of all good,
Accept our praise and bless our food.
Grace, health and strength to us afford
Through Jesus Christ, our risen Lord.
(Jeremiah Clarke)

Lord Jesus be our guest
Our morning prayer,
Our evening rest,
And with this daily food, impart,
Thy love and grace to every heart.

Be present at our table, Lord,
Be here and everywhere adored.
These creatures bless and grant that we,
May feast in paradise with thee.

All good gifts around us
Are sent from heaven above.
Then thank the Lord, O thank the Lord,
For all his love.

Take care not to get stuck on the same grace; variety will keep it more interesting. After using a set formula or pattern of words for your daily grace before meals for a little while, try making up your own. (Grace after meals too if you can manage it, although this isn't quite so important and may be difficult to keep going with younger members of the family leaving the table before the adults.) Your own prayer can be very short and simple and begin with, 'Please Father bless us and the food we are about to eat.' Later it can grow a little to express thanks for good health and family unity and prayer for the hungry of the world.

Holding hands round the table while grace is being said is very popular with the younger children. It's also very symbolic of family unity and easily leads into prayers like,

'Bless our family circle, Lord, and keep us united in your love. May we always be grateful for the food we eat and for all the good things we receive from your hand.'

TABLE PRAYERS

These are really no more than a big grace. On notable occasions, when something special is called for (for example, Christmas, Ash Wednesday, Fridays of Lent) rather than call the family together at a different and perhaps artificial time for prayers to mark the occasion, it is better to extend the grace at the evening meal or main meal of the day.

NIGHT PRAYERS

The custom of praying privately, last thing at night, continues in most Catholic families. It can be made into one of the two focal points around which family prayer can develop.

Parents can't start night prayers too early with young children. (Not, of course, merely to listen to the child reciting his prayers, but to say little impromptu prayers with and for the child.) It can begin when the baby is still in the cot with the mother or father laying her/his hand on the baby's hand and whispering gently, 'God bless our baby.' It can develop from that to a sitting/kneeling/standing beside the one-year-old's bed and saying for the child to hear, 'Thank you, Father, for taking care of us today, bless and keep us safe through the night.'

As soon as the child can benefit from a story at bedtime, night prayers can develop to include more of the family: 'Dear God please bless Martin who came to play today. Please bless too my brothers and sisters, my mummy and daddy, grandma and grandad. Please take care of me while I am asleep. Amen.'

Other concerns can, in time, be included in such prayers. Formal prayers like the 'Our Father' and 'Hail Mary' should not be introduced before the age of six, otherwise they can become nothing more than a chanted rhyme which can stand in the way of the child really learning to pray. All traditional Catholic prayers can and should be taught to the children, but only gradually and as they are old enough to understand the content of the prayer.

While it's nice to get the child to close his eyes and join his hands for prayer, there is no need to insist upon it. It is much better for the whole thing to be as natural and relaxed as possible.

KEEP GOING!

After making a resolute start the most important thing is to keep going! As with so many things where children are concerned, the motto should be 'little and often'. The grace at meal-times need only be short and to the point and night-prayers need not take long, but they must be every day.

To be a little poetic for a moment, prayer is rather like a young house plant: if it isn't watered regularly it withers and dies, but if it is cared for it will grow and beautify the house with its flowers. Prayer can only grow in people by regular practice but the effort is well rewarded. The daily talking with God, in time, beautifies a person's character and personality.

ENJOYABLE

Praying on your own or as a family group must never be allowed to become a boring chore. If it begins to get into a dreary rut try to think up ways of enlivening it. Try new approaches: read short passages from the Bible; use a book of prayers; listen to a piece of music; sing a hymn or a folk song. Any method is valid if it helps to improve the quality of your praying. If necessary, as a last resort, drop prayers together for a few days or even weeks, then make a fresh start. The only danger with that is the possibility that you will never get back to praying together.

When the children declare, 'I don't want to do it . . . it's boring,' that's not the signal for the parents to start insisting but to ask themselves, 'Is it really getting into a rut? Shouldn't we try something new?'

A priest once asked a little boy, 'Do you say your prayers every night, Jimmy?'

'Yes, Father,' Jimmy replied.

'And do you always say them in the morning too?'

'No, Father, I ain't scared in the daytime!'

Our prayers should spring from our love of God, not from fear. And God, always present and hearing and seeing all we do, does not need us to use any special pious words and language when we turn our thoughts to Him. All He wants are our hearts and minds raised to Him in love.

Earlier generations of Catholics grew up with a different attitude to prayer, repeating faithfully but mechanically every night, the same words. This resulted in a rhyming, sing-song manner of saying prayers. Even in schools prayers often turned out like that, rather like magical incantations! Unfortunately that way of doing things carried with it a kind of superstitious fear. If some of the words were missed out or you forgot to say night prayers there was the nagging anxiety that 'something' might happen to you!

We have a much more relaxed and healthy understanding nowadays. We know that our talking to God – and listening to Him – should be a natural part of our daily lives. There is no need for special pious language, dramatic gestures or posture.

Everything can and should be prayed about –

- if the children find a ladybird, they can draw it and praise God for its beauty.
- if the boy next door has an accident, we can ask God to make him better.
- if an auntie has a new baby we can thank God.
- and so on.

POSTURE

The old catechism used to say that praying was 'raising the mind and heart to God'. And that's just what it is. You can do that just as well whether you are sitting, standing, walking, lying in bed or kneeling. The advantage of introducing prayer to children while they are holding hands round the table or lying in bed is that they learn, indirectly, that a special posture is not necessary. Hopefully this will mean that the children will grow up to feel that it's quite natural to pray to their heavenly Father on the bus, in the bath, in the classroom or wherever they find themselves with a quiet moment.

TRADITIONAL PRAYERS

There's a difference between 'praying' and 'saying prayers'. The first are spontaneous little chats with God. These in time might grow to be very simply 'a raising of the heart and mind to God', without using any particular words. The second are those important set prayers or formulas which have been handed down to us over the centuries.

The 'Our Father' is, of course, the most important of these because it is the words of Jesus himself. The 'Hail Mary' must come next because it too has its roots in Scripture. These are of the first importance. The 'I believe', Memorare and others should also be taught to the children, but only when they are ready for them. One of the best ways to do this is to add a part of the Lord's Prayer or 'Hail Mary' to night prayers and gradually introduce the prayer phrase by phrase. To teach the whole prayer straight off tends to lead to a parrot-like repetition of words which might not be understood.

THE ROSARY

'And what,' the pious old parish priest asked the class of seven-year-olds, 'do you think Mary was doing when the angel Gabriel came to ask her to be the mother of Jesus?' Overawed by the venerable Irish Father the class was silent. 'Do you think she was reading a comic or lying on the floor watching television?' Silence. 'No, she was down on her knees saying her rosary!'

Well, of course, we've had the rosary a long time – but not that long! The idea of a set of prayers recited while thumbing a string of beads is found in several world religions – Buddhism, Hinduism and Islam. The title for the Christian practice is rather lovely. 'Rosary' comes from the Latin word for 'rose garden'.

The early Christian monks developed a form of the rosary but it wasn't the rosary of Our Lady as we know it today; that seems to have made its first appearance about the time of St Dominic (who died in 1221). It was not, however, officially approved by the Church until 1552 and remained very popular until the early 1960s.

The public recitation of the rosary at one time formed

an important part of parish worship but now in many places it has almost completely disappeared. This does not mean that the Church does not want us to use it privately. It would be a great shame if our children grew up ignorant of how to pray the rosary. Most children still receive a set of rosary beads on their first communion day. That presents the ideal opportunity to show them how to use their gift.

If the family is using the whole or part of the rosary at certain times of the year (May, the month dedicated to Mary, and October, the month of the rosary, perhaps) then the introduction will happen quite naturally when that time comes round. Otherwise night-prayer would seem the best time to talk about the use of the beads. A little at a time is best. There's no reason why the prayers can't be broken up or divided so as to make the whole thing more understandable. It's a love of the rosary we are trying to put across, not a regimented mechanical operation involving counting and repetition.

When a parent is saying a decade of the rosary (one is quite enough to begin with) with a child or the family together, each 'Hail Mary' can be split into its two halves, (the second part starts at 'Holy Mary . . .') each person or group having half to say. Each decade of the three Mysteries (Joyful, Sorrowful or Glorious) covers a little of the story of Christ's redeeming work and the story can be spread between the prayers. One way is to set the scene before beginning the decade ('Mary was quite young when the angel came to ask her to be the mother of Jesus. Plans were being made by her family for her to marry a carpenter called Joseph'). After the first two 'Hail Marys' the leader tells a little more of the story. This means, in practice, spreading the story over five little tellings, so it has to be done sparingly. As time goes by the children will learn what it means to meditate upon the story.

KEEP IT SIMPLE

Some families successfully turn off the TV set at a definite time each evening and kneel down for family prayers. This is very praiseworthy and excellent but there aren't too many who can do this. Some would feel that it is artificial and tends to put the children off – particularly teenagers. We must never forget that it's the *praying* that counts and the *when* and the *where* and the *how* come second. Simplicity is important. The best of all prayers are childlike, a 'Father, we love and trust you' spoken from the heart is of more value than hours of complicated prayer.

Finally
Lent is the ideal time to begin and a resolute determined start is called for. Once the first enthusiasm has worn off it is a simple matter of keeping at it. That should not mean developing a boring habit. Prayer should, as much as possible, be enjoyed by the family, and no effort or method should be spared to keep it alive and interesting. The Church's year with its festivals and seasons comes to our aid and helps to keep up our interest with its great variety.

Praying faithfully every day is to live by the Christian virtues of faith, hope and charity.

It's our *love* of God which prompts us to pray, day after day.

It's our *faith* which assures us that God is there and hears.

It's our *hope* that our loving Father will respond.

See: 1 John 4:16.

HOLY WEEK

The three very special days of the week we call 'holy' – Thursday, Friday and Sunday – are the pinnacle of the Church's year. Everything else in the year either builds up to these three days or looks back to them. They are rather like the Holy Trinity – three but one. Three days making up one event – the 'passover' of Jesus. Parents really need to read and think about all this in order to be able – over the years – to help their children understand and join fully in the celebration of Easter.

The meaning of the Easter candle, our Easter tree, even Easter eggs, will be lost if the three days are not explained and celebrated as *one* event.

The three days actually are:

Maundy Thursday evening to Good Friday evening	– Last Supper and death of Jesus.
Good Friday evening to Saturday evening	– Burial and 'silence' of grave.
Saturday evening to Easter Sunday evening	– Resurrection.

    – Jesus offers himself.
    – The offering is accepted.
    – Offering (Jesus) is given back to us.

(The Church has always followed the Jewish custom of starting the day not at sunrise but at sunset on the day before. This is how it is possible to go to Mass on Saturday evening to fulfil your Sunday Mass obligation. Saturday evening is really the beginning of Sunday.)

THE TRIUMPH OF LOVE

If you wake in the middle of the night and look out of the window it is almost as though the whole world has closed down. It's dark and silent – as silent as the grave. For the sick, nights can be long and very trying, but there's always the hope of the coming of light and the dawning of a new day.

If you take a country walk in mid-winter the trees seem dead and the countryside is bleak but there's the hope and happiness of spring to look forward to. When someone we love dies everything seems to close down – it seems to be night-time and winter-time all rolled into one. But our Christian faith tells us at such a time that there is life after death; the light and happiness of a future resurrection gives us hope.

At the dawn of each day light triumphs over darkness.
Each year spring triumphs over winter.
In every person's life love can triumph over death.

In the first two nature takes it course, in the third the co-operation of the human person is required. Love *can* triumph if it springs from a lively faith. And the basis of that faith is Christ's own triumph over suffering and death.

At the time of Jesus and throughout the lives of the Apostles the Roman Empire, which was the political power in their lives, celebrated 'triumphs'. When a general returned to Rome after a great land or sea victory there was a massive triumphant procession through the streets of Rome. The victorious general's chariot was decorated with wreaths of laurel announcing that he was the victor.

The early Christians did not hang up crucifixes in their homes as we do. When they portrayed the cross it was without the naked figure of Christ. It was shown as a triumphant sign with a laurel wreath around it. Christ had died but had risen victorious – Christ, the victor over death.

Our drawing shows the victor's laurels surmounting the cross and round the CH-RO sign. That comes from the Greek letters Xp (in English CHR) and is shorthand for Christ. So the picture – from a fourth-century sculpture – says, 'Christ, the victor, has triumphed over the cross.'

ESCAPE STORIES

A very good preparation for the children's understanding of Holy Week and the 'passover' of Jesus is a good escape story. An escape from imprisonment to freedom. Sometimes newspapers carry stories, often with accompanying pictures and drawings. Easter-time is a very popular time for escapes to be made from East Berlin, and one such escape over the Berlin wall a couple of years ago was a perfect story to discuss with the family. Such an event can bring out the tremendous drive people have to be free and what dreadful risks they will take to escape from tyranny:

John and Michael were well aware that over seventy people had been killed trying to escape over the Berlin wall but they were determined to try. With the help of a friend who lived in West Berlin they worked out a plan. First they searched for a tall block of flats on their side of the wall. It had to face a house that wasn't quite so tall on the west side of the wall. When they had found number five Schmoller Strasse, they needed a fibreglass bow, steel arrows, 100 metres of fishing line and some quarter-inch diameter steel wire.

They hid in the top of the house for fifteen hours until conditions were just right. At a signal flashed by torch from the house on the other side at 5 a.m., they opened a window and fired the arrow with the line attached over the house opposite. The arrow sailed over the house to where their friend was waiting. He pulled in the line with the cable attached to it and secured it to the back of his car. Each of the escapers had to wait for the moment when the Communist guards in their observation towers were looking the other way. Then, hitched to a pulley made to run down the wire, Michael, followed by

John, sailed over the death wall to the house on the other side, passing over the wall from the closed-in unhappiness of East Berlin to joy and freedom.

It was very like the great escape of the Israelites from the slavery of Egypt. That event has been celebrated by the Jewish people every year since it happened to this day.

The above escape story could be used in discussion with the family, although basing the discussion on a topical story straight from the newspaper would be better. To help get the idea of 'passover' across to the younger family members it might be useful to make a chart, something like this:

John and Michael feel closed in and unhappy in East Berlin.	Escape over the 'death wall'.	Freedom and new life in the West.
Moses and Israelites very unhappy slaves in Egypt.	Escape through the waters of 'sea of reeds'.	Freedom and new life in promised land.
Jesus unhappy at our slavery to sin.	Escape for us through Jesus' death.	Freedom from effects of original sin – new life as children of God.

You can well imagine John and Michael's joy and excitement at escaping and how they would celebrate every year the anniversary of their escape, their 'passing over' the 'death wall'. So every year the Jewish people celebrate their 'passing over' all those centuries ago. It is important for an understanding of so much in the Christian way of life (especially baptism and the Mass) to realise that it was on the very festival of the Passover that Jesus went out to his death and passed over to the risen life.

THE THREE SPECIAL DAYS

Every effort should be made by the whole family to attend the liturgy on these special days – the highlight of the year.

MAUNDY THURSDAY

While Jesus, as a devout Jew, celebrated the Jewish festival of Passover, he gave us, for the very first time, the sacrament and sacrifice of the Eucharist. By so doing he placed himself forever at our service.

The liturgy on this evening falls into three dramatic acts:

a) After the Gospel story of Jesus washing the feet of his friends the priest washes the feet of a number of volunteers.
b) We recall that this Eucharist celebrates the very first time Jesus gave himself in this way.
c) The altars are stripped.

If your family cannot attend the evening liturgy, then before the evening meal you could have an extended grace, your own little service. This would, of course, be adapted according to the ages of those present.

After the sign of the cross, mum or dad can ask one of the children, 'What is special about today? What happened on the first Maundy Thursday?' Trying to build on the answer, whatever it might be, mum or dad continues, 'In the Church this evening three important things happen. Everyone there will remember the first time Jesus gave himself to us in Holy Communion. They will also remember something else that he did. It was to show us that Holy Communion isn't something just for ourselves. He got up from the table (if mum is speaking then dad can get up – this is especially easy if the family is eating in the kitchen and can match the words with actions), filled a bowl with water and put a towel over his arm. Then he went round and washed the feet of his friends – including Judas who was just about to go out and betray him.' (The parent with bowl and towel may match actions with words and take off socks and briefly wash the family's feet.)

When the parent has sat down: 'Only after Jesus had shown his love in this way, by serving his friends, did he take the bread, bless it and give it to them.'

The little service can finish with a simple prayer like, 'We thank you, Lord Jesus, for your example of humble service and for the gift of yourself in the Eucharist, the breaking of bread. May we follow your example of loving and helping one another. May we always be grateful for all the gifts we receive from you. Amen.'

GOOD FRIDAY

For the modern family there is a certain tension between Good Friday as the 'holy day' and as the public holiday. On the only other occasion when a sacred day and a secular holiday come together – Christmas Day – everyone is more or less in step. However, on Good Friday the secular world is coolly indifferent to the sacred meaning of the day. If parents are serious about their Faith then there will be no question about where the emphasis will be. From the very beginning of the day it should be experienced by the family as different and special.

GOOD FRIDAY BREAKFAST

Lots of families replace their breakfast toast on this day with toasted hot cross buns. As it's a bank holiday, with a little organisation, breakfast can be all together. Whoever leads the grace should draw everyone's attention to the hot cross buns with some suitable comment like,

'Dear Father, even the food we eat today reminds us how special and important this day is. Your Son's great love and obedience took him to death on the cross; please deepen our love of you and help us to be obedient to your commandments. May we always be grateful for the food we eat and all the gifts you give us. We ask this through Jesus, who lives and reigns now and for ever. Amen.'

While we recall what happened on the first Good Friday so that we may better appreciate Jesus' great love for us, we must keep in mind that Jesus is here and now with us. His resurrection gave us his continuing presence forever. So while we recall the sad events of that day and express sorrow for our sin, we must remember that we have him with us while we recall those events!

WAY OF THE CROSS

Today, in some form or other, the story of Our Lord's passion should be followed in a devotional way. It's true that the family will hear the Passion read at the afternoon liturgy, but something additional might be attempted. This could be:

a) A service of the Way of the Cross arranged in the parish church.
b) A family version of the Way (see page 61).
c) A public procession of witness.
d) A simple retelling by parents for their children.

Those who have lived through the cold and gloom of winter really appreciate the beauty of spring. Those who have suffered the loneliness of a wakeful night greet the morning light with relief and joy.

In a similar way only those who have taken Lent seriously and died spiritually with Christ on Good Friday can experience the resurrection joy of Easter.

A PUBLIC PROCESSION OF WITNESS

In some places a united procession of witness is organised on Good Friday by the local Council of Churches. It usually involves the carrying of a large wooden cross through the streets in the middle of the day. Sometimes the procession takes the form of a Way of the Cross with regular stops for a meditation on the Passion, a Scripture reading and a prayer. Not everyone finds it easy to do but it really is a terrific opportunity for the family to proclaim their Faith. It's a wonderful annual lesson for the children, showing them the need to be courageous in witnessing to their Faith.

TELLING THE STORY

An old-fashioned recounting of the Passion in one's own words can't be improved upon. As the story is one of supreme love and sacrifice it is very fitting for it to be told in a family group. Mum or dad know enough of the story to put it across without having to read it (the Gospel Passion will be read during the afternoon liturgy).

Pictures are a different matter. They are a great help to both the parent in telling and the children in listening. One of the best sets of pictures available are those from the film 'Jesus of Nazareth'. They can be obtained as slides but the book of the same name – the text is by William Barclay – has over twenty excellent pictures on the Passion. The children need reminding, before showing them the photographs, that these are not real photos of Jesus and his friends but pictures from a film where actors take the parts. This book should be available in paperback from any good bookseller. After the 'telling' – and naturally the inevitable questions – the younger members can be encouraged to draw a picture or use playdough or building bricks to depict a part of the story.

FAMILY FAST DAY

For the adults Good Friday is a day of fasting and abstinence. But there is no more suitable day in the year for the whole family to do without a little. Before the main meal of the day the grace should reflect this:

> Almighty Father, today we are thinking about the wonderful love of Your Son which took him to the cross. That love reminds us that we often fail in our loving. To express our sorrow for the hurt we have caused you we are trying to do without a little today. Please accept the love we are trying to express in this way and may the money we save and give to the needy uplift them a little. We thank you for all the good things we have received from your hand, especially the food we are about to share. Amen.

HOLY SATURDAY

Easter Decorations. Children, especially young ones, learn better through what is seen to take place in the home than by words spoken at school, at church or even in the home. So to help the children look forward eagerly to Easter – as indeed they do to Christmas – things need to happen and be seen to happen!

We have no tradition in this country of decorating our homes for Easter but there's no reason why we cannot start our own family tradition. Children are never going to discover the importance of Easter as the pinnacle of the Church's year if it remains uncelebrated in the home. With the season of spring reflecting the theme of new life, the ideal preparation is to take a walk in the countryside or perhaps a park. Primary school children will almost certainly have been talking about spring and new life at school. But pre-school children too will take delight in being shown the daffodils in flower and the new fresh green buds appearing on the trees and bushes.

A few bunches of daffodils arranged with a selection of twigs in bud collected on your country walk (not from the park, of course!) make a simple and effective arrangement. The children are on school holidays for a few days before the festival and can be organised to decorate the house in fitting fashion. Most young children like to have the opportunity to show off their drawing and painting skills. Scenes from Nature, showing new life appearing, pictures of Easter eggs, pictures of the open tomb, of Jesus appearing to his friends – there are plenty of subjects. But no – definitely no Easter bunnies! They have absolutely no relevance or connection with Easter.

The emphasis of the pictures should be joyful and positive but if a child insists on drawing a crucifixion scene, use it as an opportunity to talk about the death of Jesus. Take care to emphasise that the sad part, when Jesus seemed to be beaten by death, was followed by the most important part of all – his coming alive in a new and special way. That new way of living makes it possible for him to be with us now, forever, as our friend. Then encourage the young artist to show the victory of Christ by adding yellow and orange rays shining out from the cross to all parts of the world.

EASTER CANDLES

In some primary schools they learn how to make Easter candles from paper. They are extremely simple and most appealing. Any home could make a number to stand among the flowers on the mantelpiece, window sill, etc. They can be as large or small as the paper supply allows.

While the smaller candles appeal especially to the five to eight-year-olds the older children might like to co-operate on a larger project – a huge family Easter candle. Every household must have a half-used roll of wallpaper in the attic, garage or understairs cupboard (if not a neighbour will surely help). The idea is identical to the above, except this one is to be 4 or 5 feet tall(!) and made to stand on its own in a dignified corner of the living room, lounge, hallway or whatever. It might be better for it to stand in a decorated tub or box. As older children are involved the candle can have closer resemblance to the Easter candle in the parish church, adding a decorated **A** and **Ω** (Alpha and Omega) and the year's date.

EASTER CARDS

If we are serious about the importance of Easter and what it means we should make an effort to send cards. There is never a very good selection in the shops for the obvious reason that there is little demand! The children could use their leisure time and talent throughout Holy Week in producing homemade ones.

EASTER EGGS

If it wasn't for Easter eggs most children would not realise that there was anything special about the Easter bank holiday weekend. At first glance they seem to have no link with Our Lord's death and resurrection but in fact they can be a most useful teaching aid. The first and most important rule about Easter eggs and their symbolism is that within the family no Easter eggs are to be given or eaten before Easter Day. (The 'Day' – 'this is the day the Lord has made' – begins with the end of the Easter vigil.) Families with young children tend to produce the eggs *after* breakfast (for obvious reasons!) on Easter morning. After breakfast, which should ideally be of boiled eggs, mum and dad can make something of the occasion by presenting the eggs with an accompanying explanation of their symbolism.

The adult needs only an ordinary hen's egg (hard-boiled) to illustrate the explanation. He could follow the general outline of the following:

'Why do we have chocolate eggs as a present today?' (Children's various answers; even if an older child remembers a previous year's explanation and gives a correct answer, still proceed with the following for the sake of any younger child.) 'Can you imagine for a moment a space ship landing from outer space? The landing site it chooses is a wide, pebbly beach. After a few minutes a hatch opens and out steps a strange-looking little space traveller. He looks around at the scenery – there's no one in sight. Bending down he picks up one of the round/oval stones. He weighs it in his hands, then tests it with a little calculator-like box in his left hand. It's smooth, cold and lifeless. He looks around at a beach full of lifeless stones. Our space traveller walks up the beach to a bank of grass. After inspecting that, he sees in the distance a farm house and its barns and outhouses. He walks cautiously towards the buildings. Halfway there he almost steps on a cluster of brown, oval, stone-like objects. "More stones," he thinks, but when he picks one up it's warm. He runs his little machine over it and finds, to his surprise, that there is life inside what looks and feels like a stone.' (The storyteller now shows the egg he/she is holding and says, 'Eggs really do look and feel like stones.')

'As the space traveller holds the egg in his hand it cracks, once, twice, three times, and as he watches a little chick pushes his head out into the world. You can imagine the surprise of the space traveller; new life from what looked like a stone. It is a perfect example of what happened on the first Easter morning. The stone, behind which Jesus had been buried, looked cold and dead, but suddenly new life burst out of it – Jesus was alive. The risen Jesus came out of what seemed a cold dead stone to new life.'

Such a story can bring out the symbolism and relevance of the chocolate Easter egg.

EASTER DAY

'This is the day,' we sing on Easter Sunday. The Day of love's triumph over sin and death. Everything about Easter Sunday speaks of triumph. Eastern Christians call it that 'unique and holy day, king and lord of days, feast of feasts, solemnity of solemnities'. It is so important a day for Christians that having prepared for it for forty days, the next forty days are spent celebrating it! For the forty days from Easter Sunday until Ascension Day, 'Alleluia' is our song as 'the day' is continually celebrated. When those forty days are up the celebration of Our Lord's resurrection continues – every Sunday; the first day of the week is our weekly remembrance of the day that He rose.

There's a neat catch question to ask children if you discover that they are learning about the ten commandments. You can ask, 'Which of the ten commandments do Christians break?' The answer is the fourth commandment, 'Remember to keep holy the Sabbath day.' Those commandments were drawn up for the Jewish people and the fourth one refers to their holy day which, of course, is Saturday. Jesus said that he had not come to sweep away the Jewish laws, but to fulfil them. This is one example where God still wants us to retain the idea behind the law, but on a different day. Christians, of course, keep Sunday holy, the first day of the week and the day Jesus rose from the dead.

SUNDAYS

With so many jobs to do around the house, in the garden and on the car, it is difficult for adults to think of Sunday as a 'holy' day. But that's what it is if being a Christian means anything to us. It is also a family day when families have the opportunity, being free from work, to be together and do things together.

'FATHER'

There should be two highlights to the day, both to do with 'family'. As members of God's family we meet together with other family members to share a meal, offer a sacrifice and celebrate Jesus' continuing presence with us. Sunday Mass is just that. There are too many of us to actually get *round* the altar table but that's what we would do if it were possible. We listen to God's word and share from the table of the Lord.

The Passover meal is the centre of the Jewish year – the Last Supper meal of Jesus has become the centre of the week for Christians: 'The Eucharist is a family meeting, a meeting of the large family of Christians. Every altar will always be a table round which gathers a family of brothers and sisters.' (Pope John Paul II.)

The second highlight of Sunday is our own private family meal together – Sunday dinner. There can be no more important family event regularly each week than this. It is so vital to the happy balanced life of the family that parents should insist, gently but firmly, that no matter what, the whole family will always be together for Sunday dinner.

All through human history sharing a meal has always been seen as a very significant thing to do. 'Going out for a meal' is still one of the most accepted ways to celebrate an anniversary or a birthday. Think too of wedding receptions, birthday parties, and so on; they are all to do with eating together. In most societies around the globe sharing a meal together denotes special bonds of friendship.

If you want to strengthen your family life then eat together as often as you can – daily if possible. The family table is the place for sharing and serving one another. Talking, sharing ideas, asking advice, passing on news, this all takes place round the table. It's difficult to think of every Sunday dinner as a celebration but good habits can be formed to make it clearly special and different. If a table-cloth isn't used during the week then on Sunday it will add to the occasion. Laying the place settings with care, arranging a simple flower display or a decorative centre-piece: simple little things can mark the meal as different.

EASTER AND 'THE TEENS'

That agonising period of development which we call, in modern jargon, 'the teens', is a time of discovery, and not only for the young person! This time of self-discovery includes searching for what is real, and what is true: 'They look for independence and are reluctant to conform. Sometimes they wish to reject past traditions and even reject their faith.' That was Pope John Paul II, speaking at York, on his first visit to Britain. He showed that he knew and appreciated this period of questioning that adolescents have to go through on their way to adulthood.

Parents often feel that they have personally failed if a son or daughter, nurtured in the Faith, suddenly and sullenly refuses to go to Mass. Parents have to be fair to themselves and realise that this rebellion is natural and quite healthy. The young person needs time and support as he/she sorts out in his mind his priorities, and finds his way, hopefully, to a more mature faith and commitment.

THE GIVING OF LOVE

Many families now have home computers and lots of them have found that using a home computer isn't that simple. If you want to get the most out of such an electronic device you have to learn basic computer-language. You need to understand the symbols and signs used, how to give instructions to the computer and understand what it says.

The same thing goes for learning to drive. If you want to be a competent driver and pass your driving test you must know and understand the road signs. The 'language' of the road consists not just in road signs shown in the highway code but also in the experience of how other people drive.

So many 'languages' exist in addition to the obvious one of the spoken word. Another example, from day to day relationships between people, is what's called 'body language' – the messages people convey to one another by the way they stand, sit and walk, or what they do. This is particularly true in the family:

'Don't you look at me like that!' the parent says to the sullen child.

'Stop lounging around and get your bedroom tidied up,' says an exasperated mother to her teenage daughter.

'This is for you,' the young child says, handing mum a dandelion.

The words of the old song sum it up:

> It's not what you do
> but the way that you do it.
> It's not what you say
> but the way that you say it.
> That's what it's all about.

There's a rather neglected little story in the first book of the Bible – Genesis 11:1–9. It goes like this:

Pride brings Disunity

At that time, some while after Noah's rescue through the ark, there was only one language spoken by all the people on earth. Then they had a very proud idea: 'Let's make a name for ourselves by building a town and a tower reaching right up into the heavens.' God, however, was not pleased with their idea and while they were busy building, He confused everything and everyone by giving them many different languages. They stopped building because they could no longer communicate with one another.

From that moment on, the Bible tells us, every tribe and people had their own language. As there was now no single language, God Himself used signs and symbols to communicate with the human race. And throughout history that is how God has – except to a few very special people – made Himself known.

GOD 'SPEAKS' THROUGH SIGNS

Of the signs God has used, fire immediately springs to mind (see page 99) but also the wind. There's the beautiful story of Elijah in the first Book of Kings 19:9–14. The prophet experiences the presence of God not in a strong wind, nor in the earthquake, nor in lightning but in a gentle breeze!

In our lives today God makes His loving presence and His actions known through the words of Scripture and the sign-language of the sacraments (see pages 106–7). If we want to understand what God is saying to us we must learn what the 'language' means and how to use it.

EACH FEAST HAS ITS SYMBOLS

Each of the Church's feasts has its symbols and signs. Christmas has the baby, the supreme sign of God's love. Epiphany has the Magi with their gifts, showing that God's love is not just for one group of people but for everyone. Easter has the special candle and the waters of Baptism.

Pentecost is especially rich in God's sign-language.

When Pentecost day came round, they had all met in one room, when suddenly they heard what sounded like a powerful wind from heaven, the noise of which filled the entire house in which they were sitting; and something appeared to them that seemed like tongues of fire; these separated and came to rest on the head of each of them. They were all filled with the Holy Spirit, and began to speak foreign languages as the Spirit gave them the gift of speech (Acts 2:1–4).

And, full of energy and courage, the Apostles rushed out into the crowded streets to speak about Jesus as Lord and saviour. All the foreigners from every corner of the Roman Empire in Jerusalem for the feast of Pentecost, were amazed to find that they could understand what was said. It was the tower of Babel story in reverse! (See page 93.) The Spirit brought unity as the Church began to be built.

THE SPECIAL MESSAGE OF PENTECOST

The signs of Pentecost are –

Wind: Now that we have the everyday use of electricity we forget how the wind was once used as a source of energy. Ships were propelled by wind and windmills ground grain and drew up water; so the blowing of the wind was a sign of the arrival of energy and power.
Fire: In our more luxurious lives we fail to realise how important fire was in simpler, more rudimentary times. It was essential for heating, cooking and lighting in the home. It was a symbol of warmth, purification and illumination. Fire also arouses widely different emotions – a cosy glow when seated round an open fire in the winter and terrifying fear when a building catches fire.

At Pentecost the Holy Spirit came as a source of great energy and power and in that power the Apostles immediately went out to proclaim Christ. Pentecost then is the birthday of the Church and the time when we are all reminded of our Christian call to be missionaries. The Apostles were transformed by the coming of the Spirit. The fire symbolised how the Spirit warmed their hearts and cleansed their minds. Putting it very simply, the penny dropped! Suddenly they understood who their friend Jesus really was and what they must do – and out they went to do it.

THE JEWISH FEAST OF PENTECOST

Long before the time of Jesus, the Jewish people had celebrated the feast of Pentecost, as they still do today. It's a celebration of the first picking from the harvest fields – rather like the Harvest festival we have later in the year. It is also closely linked to the Passover (see page 79). After Passover they counted fifty days and on the fiftieth celebrated Pentecost (the word means 'fiftieth' in Greek). It was on that day that the Jewish people celebrated the Covenant (or agreement) that God had made with Moses, their leader. It was the spirit of the Covenant, their loyalty to God, that united them.

The Christian Church actually begins with the 'passover' of Christ at Easter, but only with the coming of the Holy Spirit (while the Apostles, as good Jews, were celebrating the Jewish feast) does it really come alive. Pentecost is the completion or fulfilment of Easter. It is always thought of as the birthday of the Church.

GIVING OF LOVE

Our first chapter, 'The Coming of Love', spoke of the great revealing of Jesus in his Good News that God *is* love. At Christmas we celebrate that wonderful event when God came into our world as one of us. Our second chapter was about the Epiphany and was entitled 'The Showing of Love' because the word Epiphany means 'showing'. The chapter covering Lent and Holy Week was called 'The Offering of Love' because Jesus' love for us prompted him to make the offering of himself on our behalf to the Father. Because the Father accepted his offering Easter is a time of great triumph. So that chapter was called 'The Triumph of Love'.

This present chapter is entitled 'The Giving of Love' because true love shows itself in its impulse to give, and perfect love gives perfectly and completely.

The Holy Spirit is understood to be the spirit of love between the Father and the Son in the intimate life of the mysterious Holy Trinity. It was the giving of that same spirit of love that transformed fearful men instantly into energetic preachers and missionaries. It was the fire of love given to their hearts that warmed them and burnt out of their minds their misunderstandings about Jesus and his message.

THE NEGLECTED FESTIVAL

As the fulfilment of Easter and the birthday of the Church, this day is one of the most important in the year. It is certainly more important than Christmas, yet it is rather neglected. This might be because of the time of the year – warmer weather and holidays in the air; it might be because the symbols of the feast are not so easy to under-stand; it could be because the secular bank holiday weekend of Whitsun gets confused with the Christian

Whit Sunday, or it may be because its importance has never properly been understood and no tradition has been built up. For whatever reason, it is the 'Cinderella' of the three major festivals (that's not to say that the other two are ugly!). Our parish churches could do more to mark the Church's birthday and to encourage the celebration of the occasion in the home.

WHICH NAME, WHITSUN OR PENTECOST?

A worthwhile little project to set the children as part of their preparation for Pentecost is to ask them to find out – from school or their local priest or possibly from the library or from books around the home – what is the meaning of the two names given to this time in the Church's year. It is amazing how few Catholics know what either word means or how to use it.

First, it has to be said that both titles do apply to the self-same day. As we said above, the name 'Pentecost' comes from the Jewish tradition and means 'fiftieth day' since the Passover. The word 'Whitsun' is a shortening of 'Whitsunday' and is totally of Christian origin. In the early Church the period from Easter to Pentecost, during which Easter continued to be celebrated, was the time when people who had prepared throughout Lent to be received into the Christian community were baptised. In our part of the world, Northern Europe, it became more common and popular to have the baptisms at or near Pentecost day. (This may have been because of the climate – the candidates for baptism had to strip off! See page 45.) In England the feast became known as 'White Sunday'. This was because of the white clothes worn after their baptising by the newly received converts. Naturally in time this was broken down to 'Whit Sunday' and 'Whitsun'.

CHILDREN AND SYMBOLS

Pentecost is a perfect time to introduce or re-introduce the children to signs and symbols. Here are some symbols that are associated with the festival. Get the children to draw and colour them.

The descending dove. This symbol is associated with and drawn from the times the Holy Spirit was active in Our Lord's life, e.g. Matthew 3:16.

Tongues of fire. Seven are drawn to tie in with the seven gifts of the Holy Spirit that are a result of His coming. (Acts 2:1–4.)

The wind is not easy to symbolise but the children might like to draw a windmill, or instead make this paper windmill. It could be decorated with the two symbols from above.

Here are a few other symbols of the Resurrection that the children might like to draw and give you the opportunity to explain!

The Butterfly

It's not only children that find it fascinating how the caterpillar goes into a cocoon (a type of tomb) where it seems to die, then emerges to a new life as a beautiful butterfly. It is a terrific symbol of Christ's death and resurrection. Rather than skip over this symbol quickly it might be an idea to have a more detailed home project based on different butterflies and their life cycles. Don't forget to point out the symbolism; it is a most valuable way of tying in God's creation with His work of re-creation.

The Phoenix

This was a very popular symbol of the Resurrection with the early Christians. They used it on burial stones and in their writings. The first Christian writer that we know of who used the ancient legend about a mythical bird was Clement of Rome. Around AD 98 he gives the legend in his letter to the Corinthian Christians and applies it to the resurrection of all Christ's faithful followers. Later it was applied to Christ's own resurrection.

According to legend the phoenix was a bird that lived for

500 years, then built itself a funeral pyre for a nest and burnt itself to death. When the ashes cooled the bird rose again from the ashes to start a new life.

Lamb and Flag

At the time of Jesus lambs were sacrificed in the Jerusalem temple as part of an act of worship. Jesus was described by John the Baptist as 'the lamb of God'; the lamb that would be sacrificed to take away the sins of the world. Only this lamb was victorious, rising to a new life. The standing lamb then represents Jesus and the flag is the sign of his triumph.

LOVE IS

As Pentecost is the time when we recall the giving of the Spirit of Love to the Church, the table prayer for the principal meal can be based on the theme of love in the family. There is a well-known series of individual cartoon pictures captioned, 'Love is . . .' They appear every day in one of the national newspapers. Examples are:

'Love is sharing problems with each other,' with a picture of daddy and mummy sitting talking.

And 'Love is giving the children swimming lessons,' with a drawing of daddy holding a child up in the water at the local pool, while another child sits on the edge.

It should be quite easy to get hold of two or three suitable samples. Show them to the family in the week before

Whitsun and suggest that they secretly (a little confidential help from mum may be needed!) draw a picture for each member of the family. For example, one of the children might draw mum cuddling a child with the caption, 'Love is giving us a cuddle when we don't feel very well.' Or for dad there might be a picture of a car with two feet sticking out from underneath, with the words, 'Love is making the car safe for us all.' Mum and dad could enter into the fun and draw a suitable picture (matchstick people are good enough!) for each of the family. Each person's cartoons can be out of sight until the morning of Pentecost day and then placed, folded, at each person's place for breakfast. The grace could be something like:

> Today we recall that wonderful moment when the Holy Spirit, the Spirit of Love, came upon the Apostles. They were filled with energy and fired by love. May that same Spirit fill us with energy in God's service and love for one another.

Then everyone opens up their pictures and enjoys a laugh when the secrets are revealed! They might be used to decorate the kitchen for the following week and be a talking point for neighbours and friends that call.

Children love candles and especially blowing them out. Later in the day at the principal meal – if candles can be obtained – everyone can have one in front of their place at table. At grace-time mum or dad can say something like,

> 'At birthday parties there's usually a birthday cake with candles. Today is the birthday of the Church. When we were baptised we became God's people, members of His Church. We are the Church and the candles in front of us are like the ones we were each given when we were baptised. Today it is a birthday candle.' (The candles can now be lit.) 'Your candle

flames are like the tongues of fire which were seen over the heads of the apostles on the first Pentecost day. Let us be quiet, just for a moment, and ask the Holy Spirit to come and fill our hearts with the fire of his love.' Short pause. 'Now let's blow out our candles.' To conclude, 'When the apostles had received the Holy Spirit they rushed out to tell everyone about Jesus. We are missionaries too and in our own little way we must try and make God's love known. So now we say, "Thank you God for the love we share in this home and family. Thank you too for the food which comes from your loving hand." Amen.'

If mum has led the above dad might like to finish off with a reading of the following passage. If dad led the table prayer perhaps the eldest child could read it. (It's not for mum to read out!) It needs to be introduced with a remark like, 'A fourteen-year-old girl was asked at school to write about a missionary she knew, and this is what she wrote.'

A Missionary I know

When I was asked to write about a missionary I knew, a few people crossed my mind, such as Mother Teresa, then I stopped and thought, 'I can't write about one of these great people because I don't really know them. It's true I've heard their names and read and been told about them, but I don't know what they're like.'

The person I think is a missionary, and a good one, is my mother. This may sound peculiar but surely you don't have to be ordained to be a missionary. My mum's mission is to be a housewife and a mother to me and my family. My mum has never been selfish and put herself first before her family. I have never been starved or been without her endless love. Just like the famous missionaries, my mother has needed a lot of courage. She could easily have gone off to bingo and left me, but she didn't. She made the supreme sacrifice of thinking about me before herself. I am very lucky to have a missionary mother.

If there are teenage children in the family an interesting exchange of ideas might develop over the meal after that school essay.

EASTER SACRAMENTS

The special fifty days from Easter to Pentecost is the period when, traditionally, the three sacraments of Baptism, Confirmation and Holy Communion have been given. We have spoken repeatedly about baptism because it is so important.

CONFIRMATION

'They can't leave anything alone, can they! I don't know what they're doing to confirmation but when I was a youngster the bishop came round every three years and we were confirmed when we were eight or nine.'

There's definitely been a re-think in the Church about confirmation, and in fact the thinking goes on! The sacrament is now delayed till an age when the young person can understand more fully what it's all about and decide for himself if he wants to be an adult member of the Church. Confirmation, as we shall see, completes baptism. As the baby could not make a commitment, at confirmation the young person, if not too young, will be able to. ·

CONFIRMATION IN THE EARLY CHURCH

The changes we've seen in recent years have come from a better understanding of how the sacrament fitted into the order of things in the early Church. Quite simply (see page 53), Lent was used as the time for preparing the new recruits to the Church. When they had been instructed and prepared they were received into the community. This would have been on Easter Night or during the fifty days that followed. But they weren't just baptised, they were also confirmed and made their first Holy Communion, all at the same special occasion. That seems rather odd to us because we have been brought up with the practice that evolved much later, in the Middle Ages. It seems that in the first three to four hundred years of the Church's life it went something like this: The baptism (see page 45) was conducted privately, apart from where the congregation were gathered. This was because of the custom of the person entering the water naked, the new convert being anointed with oil and given special new white clothes as he left the water. Then the new Christians were taken to the assembled congregation where they were presented to the community as its new members and given a rousing welcome. The bishop, who would have been presiding, formally received the new members by laying his hands on their heads. While doing this he prayed that they would receive an outpouring of the Holy Spirit. This was followed by an anointing of their heads to show that they now belonged to Christ (the word 'Christ' means 'the anointed one') and were 'Christians'. Then everyone present would celebrate the Eucharist and the new Christians received Holy Communion for the first time.

This 'confirming' ceremony became, in time, the separate sacrament of Confirmation. The two sacraments became separated when the practice of baptising babies developed.

Notice the sign-language of confirmation – the laying on of hands by the bishop and the sign of the cross with holy oil. The first was used in Old Testament times by the great figures, such as Abraham and Isaac, who used to pass on a blessing to their sons with this sign. At the time of Jesus a religious teacher would lay his hands on the heads of those he was about to send out to teach.

THE SIGN-LANGUAGE OF THE SACRAMENTS

As the risen Jesus, alive and with us, is not visible, we need clear signs to show when he is touching our lives in a special way. For example, the way Christ can act as our daily strength comes across clearly in our receiving the bread (and sometimes the wine) of Holy Communion. That's a sign that actually contains what it's signifying.

The waters of baptism convey the idea of washing clean, but also of the giving of new life. The anointing with oil in baptism, confirmation, holy orders and in the sacrament for the sick is a sign of being made 'special' or set apart. In Old Testament times only priests and kings were anointed in such a way. And, of course, Jesus received the title of 'the Christ', which means 'the anointed one'. Being a 'Christ-ian' sets us apart in the world with a special task to witness to Christ (hence the importance of things like the procession of witness, see page 82).

SACRAMENTS IN THE FAMILY

None of the sacraments are purely private meetings with Christ. They all involve us as members of God's family. That's why when a child receives the sacrament of Penance for the first time, or Holy Communion or Confirmation, the preparation and the celebration must be, as much as possible, a family event.

When there's a child to be brought for Baptism the parents need to think about the meaning of the sign-language of that sacrament, and be clear about the responsibilities they are taking on. Later, when the same child is receiving the sacraments of Holy Communion and Confirmation that fulfil Baptism, the family again needs to be fully involved. They will be complementing what the school and the parish are doing to explain the meaning of the 'language' to the child. Most parishes now have schemes which set out to involve the parents in such a way, and continue to give a development in Christian knowledge after the sacraments have been received.

MARY, THE MOTHER OF THE CHURCH

Luke, who wrote the Acts of the Apostles, tells us that Mary, the mother of Jesus, was present in the upper room when the Holy Spirit came. It was very fitting that she, who had given birth to the Saviour, should be present at the birth of the Church, through which we would meet the Saviour. This is probably why Mary was declared, at the time of the Second Vatican Council, the Mother of the Church.

Much of the fifty day period following Easter comes in May which has been regarded for centuries as Mary's month. Many grandparents will remember the May processions that were held in most parishes up until the early 1960s. The processions were out of doors, often through the streets of the parish carrying a large statue of Mary, with the public recitation of the rosary and Marian hymns. At that time it was very common for children to have their own little May altars in the home. There would be a statue of Our Lady and a simply arranged bunch of flowers.

Whatever the value of the outdoor processions, there is no doubt that the children's devotion and love and respect for Mary during May was valuable and to be encouraged. It is something we can do well to continue and can be so simply arranged. The children will love finding and arranging flowers for their 'altar'. It's another 'occasion' and opportunity for prayer together. A decade of the rosary, in the simple way already explained (see page 72), would flow naturally and valuably.

THE LIVING OF LOVE

'If you do that once more I'll . . .'
'How many times must I tell you . . .'

Living out love in the family is a constant uphill struggle!
Clearing up after the children, keeping after them to get
ready, get washed and get a move on, sorting out their
squabbles, tolerating their noise and so on and so on! No
other way of life offers so much aggravation and tempt-
ation nor, on the other hand, such an opportunity to grow
in patience and maturity. It's a giving of oneself, and
giving and giving . . . If we look at it all positively it's an
opportunity for a steady growth in unselfish love. The old
song comes to mind:

'Love is something, if you give it away, give it away,
give it away,
Love is something, if you give it away, you end up
having more.'

Marriage and family life offers just as many opportunities
for holiness as any other way of life – some would say
many more! As Pope John Paul II has said, 'Christian
marriage is the pathway to holiness for all members of a
family.'

Night feeds, getting in and out of bed countless times and stumbling around in semi-darkness to attend a sick or restless child, can be a crucifying experience, especially if it goes on night after night for months on end. But it's an experience that's at the very heart of Christianity. It's a living out of the Easter theme of dying to oneself in the service of others.

To give time to another person is to give something of oneself because we have nothing more precious to give. 'Whatever you do for the least person you do for me,' Jesus said. Therefore to help and serve one another in the family is to do things for Christ himself. When things are going badly and mum or dad is at screaming-pitch it is encouraging if in a short moment of quiet they can recall that every effort in love for the family is an effort and a mark of love for Christ.

When Pope John Paul II said, 'We are the Easter people,' he was saying that our Faith is built on the resurrection of Jesus, but more than this he was saying that it is the Easter event that makes sense of life; what is important is not just what we believe but how we live each day. All day long families have difficulties and problems and come out of them: 'I can't find my school tie'; 'I've backed the car into the garage wall!'; periods of family sickness, a family squabble, and making-up again. Individually into sin and then reconciliation with God and one another. If we have the eyes of faith to see it, life is filled with the continual cycle of 'death and resurrection' and the sustaining love of the risen Jesus.

RE-CREATION AND LOVE

Time is God's precious gift to us. It is vital for the growth of family togetherness that as much time as possible be spent together. This means naturally making the most of weekends and especially holidays. Everyone needs some

kind of break from daily routine for a rest and a change.
Only by breaking the familiar pattern of daily life can we
get a sense of re-creation, of being renewed and refreshed.
Recreation is essential and an opportunity for the family
to be united in common interests and good old straight-
forward fun.

Only by being in one another's company for a con-
tinuous week or two can there be sufficient opportunity for
the growth in love that comes from sharing. It's not only
important for each member of the family to give and share
love but it's equally important for each member to feel
that they are loved – to discover that they are lovable. No
one is able to discover all by himself his own lovableness.
While this is true for everyone, it is vitally important for
the teenager.

Within the family no masks need to be worn, no dramatic act is required, no pretence is expected. Everyone can
be themselves, always welcomed and loved. This is one of
the gifts of the Holy Spirit to the family, the ability to make
each other feel special. And *special* in spite of any recurring
naughtiness or weakness. To 're-create' together is to help
that 'specialness' grow. The summer holidays provide
such an opportunity when everything is more leisurely
and there's time for one another.

SAINTS' TIME

Through the summer months, in the Church's liturgy we
are continually looking back through Pentecost to Easter.
This is the time of the year when we notice the saints, those
members of the family of God who lived heroic lives of love
and are now with God. We are still struggling to live a life
of love but saints are people who have struggled and
with God's grace succeeded, moreover they are now in a
position to help us live the same life.

Young people need mature, unselfish adults to look up

to and admire, and this is always a challenge to parents.
But they also need heroes from outside their family. The
summer holidays provide an opportunity to introduce the
family to the Christian heroes of the past. One way is to
encourage summer holiday reading based on the lives of
the saints – the more exciting ones of course!

> The story goes that a little girl was with her family in a
> party being shown around one of our great cathedrals.
> As the guide was explaining a historic tomb nearby, the
> girl was staring at a great stained glass window through
> which the summer sun was streaming, bathing the
> cathedral floor in colour. As the group was about to
> move on she asked the guide in a shrill clear voice, 'Who
> are those people in the pretty window.'
>   'Those are the saints,' the man replied.
>   That night as she was undressing for bed she told her
> mother, 'I know who the saints are.'
>   'Do you dear?' replied her mother, 'who are they?'
>   'They're the people who let the light shine through.'

What a perfect way of describing the saints. They are the
people through whom the light of God's immense love
shines out on others.

IN THE LOCAL CHURCH

It's easy to attend the same church week after week and
take for granted and accept what's in it as part of the
decor. Quite often there are statues of saints which are
never explained to the children. (Not infrequently adults
too don't know who the saints are or anything about
them.) Nowadays there are fewer statues of the saints in
our churches but where they exist the children of the
parish should grow up knowing about them. This is
particularly true of the parish's patron saint. The children

should be encouraged to ask questions. Why, for example, do we consider St Therese of Lisieux a saint? What did St John Fisher or St Thomas More do to merit sainthood? What can we learn about living the life of love from their lives? These are questions that the parish clergy and teachers can help parents with, and ideal material for a home-based project.

HOLIDAY EXPEDITIONS

Our great cathedrals are obvious places for a family visit, but our old parish churches (the principal Anglican church in each town or village) are worth considering too. If the weather's bad while on a holiday at the seaside or at a farm, why not seize the opportunity to explore the neighbourhood and look out for one of the old pre-Reformation parish churches. Every village and town has its Anglican parish church, very many of which were built as Catholic churches and used for centuries by Catholics.

While the children might find the idea of visiting old churches a bit 'boring', it can be made interesting. For example, they can be asked to imagine the travelling craftsmen, called journeymen, who with great skill carved the wood and worked the stone for the churches. The children can be asked to imagine the stream of people, in the various period costumes, coming and going for weddings, baptisms and funerals. They can be asked to explore the church (in a dignified way) and find which parts are the really old bits (so many churches were extended or partially rebuilt over the centuries). And they can look for the clues which tell you that in this particular church Mass was once said. One of the sure signs is the existence of a piscina on the right hand side of the altar (as you face it from the body of the church). This was a little saucer-like basin with a drain-hole. Water used at Mass was poured away down this drain.

OUR ENGLISH HERITAGE

It's a wonderful opportunity to talk with the children about our national and spiritual heritage. They need to realise that being a Catholic-Christian is not just a here-and-now experience. We have roots that go way back to the conversion of England, long before AD 1066. We are members of a great spiritual family that includes hundreds of inspiring English saints. There are the ordinary people too, who once used these old churches, and who had their struggles to live a life of love and are now 'saints' with God. They are happy to pray for us who are still struggling. So while we admire the craftsmanship of those long-dead Christians we should remind the children that the stained glass windows that they see, the stonework, wall paintings and other beautiful things were all made with loving care by people who shared the same Faith with us.

WALL PAINTINGS

Children might find it particularly interesting to paint or draw the wall paintings in the old parish churches. These share a direct simplicity with their own pictures. All medieval churches were more or less completely painted. Sadly, so many of these pictures have disappeared, either because they were deliberately destroyed at the Reformation or when the church was altered or enlarged they had to come down. A number of pictures have survived because in some places during the Reformation they were covered with lime-wash rather than destroyed. Some more were lost in the time of Queen Victoria because at that time there was a great craze for stripping the plaster walls to show off the original stonework. This was really a great mistake because not only were hundreds of wall pictures hidden under the lime-wash lost, but the original stonework was nothing special to look at. The original builders had never intended it to be seen!

The travelling painter of the Middle Ages was commissioned to paint on the walls of the parish church for two reasons, devotional and educational. There were no printed books. The very few that existed had been copied by hand by the monks. Because of this only about 10% of the population could read. But everyone could understand pictures and the wall pictures were aids for the teaching of the people. The priest, in his sermon, could point at a picture and speak of the Bible character shown or the saint portrayed. The pictures had to be self-explanatory and were painted with a direct simplicity. The standard of the artist's work was not very high (the better-skilled journeymen were fully employed at the cathedrals) but that didn't matter to the parishioners. The pictures were not intended to last anyway, they could easily be replaced the next time the journeyman came that way again.

There are five basic subjects covered by the pictures:

a) Bible stories
b) Single figures of saints
c) Lives of the saints
d) Moral illustrations
e) Decorative schemes

It has often been said that the people of those early English churches did not know their Bible (relative to the fact there were no printed books and hardly anyone could read) but the surviving wall paintings tell a different story. Scenes from the Bible abound, but they seem to have preferred New Testament stories. (Rather like modern Catholics!)

The single saints portrayed were, of course, those popular at the time. These were, for example, St Christopher, St Catherine, St Nicholas and St Margaret. The lives of the saints were often portrayed in a series of pictures not unlike our modern strip-cartoon. Not surprisingly one of the most popular subjects for these series was Our Lady to whom devotion was very strong in the Middle Ages.

The wall paintings were also used to warn congregations about the last judgement and the final coming of Christ. The struggle between good and evil, the promise of heaven and the doom awaiting those who die in sin are all clearly spelt out.

WHERE SOME OF THESE WALL PAINTINGS CAN BE SEEN

If you are on holiday at one of the following seaside resorts you might visit the old parish churches in the nearby village or town: If you are staying at Hastings, visit the parish church of Battle; at Brighton, then visit Patcham (there is a Sussex group of churches at Clayton, Plumpton, Hardham and Coombes which have lives of the saints in series). There are also churches at –

Eastbourne: Rotherfield	Weymouth: Cerne Abbas
Deal or Dover: Barfreston	Poole: Cranborne
Caister: Hemblington	Hartlepool: Pittington
Folkstone: Newington	Isle of Wight: Shorwell and
Penzance: Breaze	Godshill

These are only examples; a little research in your local library will reveal others.

Or perhaps near your home (for an afternoon's car ride and exploration) you could visit these:

Peakirk in Cambridgeshire	Charlwood in Surrey
Corby Glen in Lincolnshire	Stoke Dry in Leicestershire
Fairstead in Essex	East Wellow in Hampshire

And there are very many others. Has your own town or village an old parish church with a wall painting?

STAINED GLASS WINDOWS

Some beautiful stained glass still remains from the Middle Ages, but not much. Most of it was deliberately smashed by those opposed to Catholicism. This was especially true of the period of Cromwell and the Puritans. But it is still very worthwhile for the family to go out of its way to look for the early glass with its Bible stories and pictures of the saints. The best glass is to be found in the cathedrals of Canterbury, Lincoln and York Minster. Among a number of other places very old stained glass can be found in the parish churches at the following:

Brabourne and Westwell in Kent
Madley and Fladbury in Herefordshire
Stanton Harcourt and Horspath in Oxfordshire
Harlow and Margaretting in Essex
Bampton and Doddiscombsleigh in Devon
St Kew and St Neots in Cornwall
Minster and Selby Abbey in North Yorkshire
Trysull and Okeover in Staffordshire

And there's the Stained Glass Museum, North Triforium, Ely Cathedral.

While you are in these old parish churches look out for other points of interest, for example the Saxon and Norman fonts that can be found in some places.

A 'SAINTS' PROJECT

An interest to absorb some holiday time and energy for children of junior-school or lower-secondary age might be a project on saints. A scrap book each, drawing paper etc. and the challenge to find out all they can about saints, the only limitation being that *all* the material – drawings of wall pictures, information about stained glass windows, etc. – must all come from inside old churches (libraries etc. are not allowed!).

PERSONAL PATRON SAINTS

It is an old Catholic tradition to name children after canonised saints so that the child has a heavenly patron throughout life. Most Catholic parents still follow this custom although they may well have chosen the name because they like the sound of it or because it's popular in the family. While they are not likely to think about it very often, it is good for the children to know a little about the saint whose name they have been given. Each saint has a special feast-day (although not all of these are shown on the Church's calendar) and this can be kept each year by the family.

THE FAMILY'S OWN CALENDAR

In every Catholic's year there are three days which call for personal celebration. The first is the one that everyone remembers – the birthday; the second is the anniversary-day of christening and the third is the feast-day of the patron saint. So, for an imaginary little boy called Peter, his birthday could be 18th February, his christening day could have been 28th March and his feast day would be 29th June. Three days each year to recall and celebrate.

In a family of five people – mum and dad and three children – that gives a total of fifteen days each year to remember. These can be worked out and entered on the calendar that most families have hanging in the kitchen. The dates of the children's baptism will be. on their certificates and a little help from the local library, the school or the parish priest might be necessary to get the dates of the patron saint's feast-day.

It's a good idea to make a separate and special 'family celebration calendar'. This can be done in a number of ways but the easiest is to collect the liturgical calendar published and issued free by *The Universe* newspaper (this appears in the issue of the paper two or three weekends before Christmas) and adapt it. It gives all the important dates in the Church's year and you can simply add the family's dates to that. It's advisable to hang it up on the inside of a cupboard door in the kitchen because otherwise, being newsprint, it would discolour very quickly.

Another method is to get a large sheet of paper and draw it up with boxes for the dates, allowing a big border round the edge for the children to decorate. (They might like to use some of the symbols we spoke of earlier, see page 100.) The 'boxes' can be arranged in date order or in columns like this:

	Birthday	Baptismal day	Saint's day
Mum	5th April	12th May	17th November
Dad	20th May	1st July	13th June
Helen	21st February	18th April	18th August
Peter	18th February	28th March	29th June
David	5th November	12th December	1st March

These special family days can be celebrated with an appropriate grace at meal-times and the children might like to make a card to mark the day.

NEW BEGINNINGS

Before we arrive at the feast-day of all the saints we have the 'back-to-school' month of September. Because there's a kind of new beginning in early September with the start of the new school year and parish societies and groups opening up again after the summer break, it's an ideal opportunity to make a new start in the family. (To make any real progress, life has to be 'lifted' by these occasional efforts at renewal.)

It may be that you would like to begin saying grace at meal times, or perhaps follow one or two of the ideas in this book. If you feel you need an opportunity to get things going this is one of several natural starting points in the course of the year. There's the beginning of the new school year, the first Sunday of Advent, 1st January, the beginning of Lent – all 'new beginning' days when there's a reason to make a fresh start.

OCTOBER ROSARY

Each month in the Church's year is dedicated to a theme. Those which stand out are, May, the month of Our Lady, June, dedicated to the Sacred Heart, October dedicated to the rosary and November to the Holy Souls. Family prayer in October should include from time to time, if possible, the rosary. There's no need to say more than the youngest member of the family can cope with (see page 72 when we spoke of simple ways of praying the rosary).

NOVEMBER – MONTH OF THE WIDER FAMILY

November brings a reminder that we are all members of the same very big family. We know well enough that at baptism we become children of God and members of the Christian family – God's own world-wide family. This is something we 'know' but only very rarely realise and recall. But November reminds us that the family not only reaches over national boundaries but also beyond the grave. The saints in heaven and the holy souls in purgatory have faced the same challenge of living the life of love we now face. They have struggled with their own self-love and have either courageously won or have needed their love purified before they could have union with 'Love' itself. With the saints and the souls in purgatory we share the same baptism and the same calling. On 1st November we recall the saints, whether officially canonised or not, and ask them to pray for us, as we make our own pilgrimage through life. On the next day, and throughout November, we remember the souls of the departed and pray for them to be soon released from their purification and united with our loving Father.

HALLOWEEN

You can't miss All Saints' Day (or All Hallows as it was once called) because it's the only holy day in the year announced by all the children and proclaimed by an evening based on pagan superstition. In early medieval times the evening of All Hallows was a special holy time of preparation for the next day's feast. In the Celtic and Anglo-Saxon period the same date was the day before the start of their New Year. It was an occasion to placate the spirits of the dead and drive away evil spirits. The pagan goings-on on that day so heavily influenced the Christian festival of All Hallows Eve that gradually the religious connection was lost.

Irish immigrants to the United States introduced the idea over there. The Americans loved it and the customs of the evening were developed. It has returned to this country as an evening for fun and an opportunity to dress up. There's no harm done as long as there's no sign of the children taking it too seriously and the very young and sensitive are not alarmed and frightened by the masks and ghoulish attire.

ALL SAINTS' DAY

This day cannot pass without a special grace or table prayer. And it's an opportunity for any pictures from a summer research on saints (see pages 116–17) to be put up in the kitchen or elsewhere in the house. If the children have statues or pictures of their own patron saints they might like to arrange a few flowers in front of them as a mark of love and respect.

CHRIST THE KING

We end the Church's year on a note of confidence and triumph. Jesus is alive and with us; he lives by faith in our hearts. We belong to him and he belongs to us. He is our king.

Time has caught up with us again but we need never fear its passing. Christ our King is Lord of time and love. Our whole year has been passed in the light of one day, Easter Sunday, which alone ties together and makes sense of everything we have tried to do.

The children can be reminded today of the visit to the stable of the Magi (or kings) and of how, with their gifts, they foretold that Jesus would be a king. We can draw the children's attention too to the 'O' antiphon (see page 25) which proclaims Jesus 'King of the Nations' if there's an opportunity that prayer could be used today.

As this feast-day always comes on a Sunday – the last Sunday of the Church's year – it's not difficult to make something of Sunday teatime. This could be made a little different with a crown cake (described on page 27). At that meal, or at Sunday dinner, the grace could be a special one; something like this, perhaps:

Almighty Father, every day we pray that your kingdom may come.

We believe that Jesus, our risen Lord, lives by faith in our hearts. May he reign there as king and may his kingdom come in this home and family.

We thank you now for this food which we are about to share. May we be always grateful for your Fatherly care. Amen.

THE COMING OF LOVE

Next Sunday is the first Sunday of Advent when we start the Church's year all over again. In the next seven days we need to think about the Advent wreath, the Advent calendar, resolutions perhaps, and so on. But what we really require is a deep realisation of our daily need for love and of how He is always longing to come and be one with us.

INDEX